PRAYER
101

Experiencing the Heart of God

WARREN W. WIERSBE

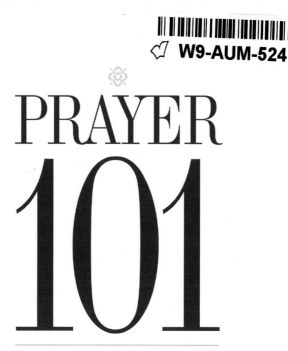

Victor®

The Bible Teacher's Teacher

COOK COMMUNICATIONS MINISTRIES
Colorado Springs, Colorado • Paris, Ontario
KINGSWAY COMMUNICATIONS LTD
Eastbourne, England

Victor® is an imprint of
Cook Communications Ministries, Colorado Springs, CO 80918
Cook Communications, Paris, Ontario
Kingsway Communications, Eastbourne, England

Prayer 101: Experiencing the Heart of God
© 2006 by Warren W. Wiersbe

First printing, 2006
Printed in the United States of America

2 3 4 5 6 7 8 9 10 Printing/Year 10 09 08 07 06

Cover Design: Two Moore Designs / Ray Moore

ISBN-13: 978-0-7814-4189-6
ISBN-10: 0-7814-4189-7

Dedicated to our prayer partners around the world who have undergirded us and our ministry for over fifty years.

Warren and Betty Wiersbe

CONTENTS

&

PREFACE

෪

What the *Book of Common Prayer* says about marriage can readily be applied to Christian prayer as well: "[It] is not to be entered into lightly or carelessly, but reverently and in the fear of God."

In today's vernacular, the phrase "reverently and in the fear of God" simply means *prayer is serious business.* After all, true praying means communing with the God of the universe and cooperating with Him in accomplishing His will on earth. If I were invited to speak to the president of the United States in the White House or to royalty in Buckingham Palace, I would feel highly honored and would prepare myself to be at my best. Should I feel any less honored or be any less prepared when I meet my heavenly Father and my Savior at the throne of grace? Prayer should be a joyful fellowship, but it's also a serious encounter, and I want to approach His throne with reverence and godly fear.

The prophet Malachi may have had a similar thought in mind when he rebuked the temple priests for offering the Lord cheap sacrifices:

"When you bring blind animals for sacrifice, is
that not wrong?
When you sacrifice crippled or diseased animals,
is that not wrong?
Try offering them to your governor! Would he be
pleased with you?
Would he accept you?" says the LORD Almighty.
(Mal. 1:8)

Prayer is not only serious business, but it's also an expensive privilege. Why should our prayers be like the cheap temple sacrifices of which Malachi speaks when Jesus had to suffer and die just to make the privilege of prayer possible? For believers to enter the Holy of Holies to speak to the Lord cost Jesus His life on the cross. It wasn't His teaching or His miracles that tore the veil of the temple from top to bottom and opened the "new and living way" (Heb. 10:20). The veil was opened because Jesus shed His blood for our sins.

To make light of prayer and take it for granted, to pray carelessly and flippantly, is to make light of the death of God's only Son. God doesn't answer cheap prayers.

SEMESTER I

ESSENTIAL PRAYER 101

૪૭

He who has learned to pray has learned the greatest secret of a holy and a happy life.

—WILLIAM LAW

Prayer is the most important thing in my life. If I should neglect prayer for a single day, I should lose a great deal of the fire of faith.

—MARTIN LUTHER

I'd rather be able to pray than to be a great preacher; Jesus Christ never taught His disciples how to preach, but only how to pray.

—DWIGHT L. MOODY

Defining a Mystery

ॐ

"We all *know* what light is," Samuel Johnson told his friend
James Boswell, "but it is not easy to *tell* what it is." He might
have said the same thing about prayer, although Boswell tells us
that Johnson said that "to reason philosophically on the nature
of prayer was very unprofitable." Ponder that statement.

What, after all, is prayer? Can we define it? Do we really
have to define it? And, if God is an all-powerful God, why
doesn't He just do what needs to be done? Does He really need
our help, through prayer, to accomplish these things? And, if
He's an all-knowing God, why do we need to pray at all? Even
Jesus taught that the Father knows what we need before we ask
Him (see Matt. 6:8), so why ask? If He's a loving God and knows
what we need, must He wait for us to pray before He can act on
our behalf? Is God our servant?

The more you think about prayer and try to explain it, the
more baffling it becomes. It reminds me of the fable of the
centipede and the beetle. The beetle asked the centipede,
"How do you know which legs to move next?" The centipede

replied, "To tell the truth, I've never thought much about it." And the more the centipede pondered the question, the more confused it became, until finally it was so bewildered that it became paralyzed.

To make things even more challenging—and I have a good reason for asking this, so please be patient—how does God, who dwells in eternity, relate to the prayers of His people, which are offered in the midst of time? Did He decree the prayers' answers even before the creation of the world? How do we define time and eternity? "What, then, is time?" Augustine asked. "I know well enough what it is, provided nobody asks me; but if I am asked what it is and try to explain it, I am baffled" (*Confessions*, Bk. 11, sec. 14). Both the lowly centipede and the great bishop warn us that, in some matters, analysis can lead to paralysis.

The esteemed devotional writer Oswald Chambers pondered these questions and wrote, "We are all agnostic about God, about the Spirit of God, and prayer. It is nonsense to call prayer reasonable; it is the most super-reasonable thing there is" (*Shade of His Hand*, p. 97). Note his careful choice of words: Prayer is not *un*reasonable but *super*-reasonable, that is, *above the greatest thoughts we might think*. Like faith, hope, love, joy, and a host of other precious spiritual and emotional experiences, prayer can't be put into a beaker and carried into the laboratory to be tested—but that doesn't make it any less real. To quote Chambers again, "Prayer is not logical, it is a mysterious moral working of the Holy Spirit" (*Christian Discipline*, vol. 2, p. 51).

So, from the unbeliever's point of view the question is, "Why pray?", but from the believer's point of view the question is, "Why *not* pray?" We're the children of God, and as such we need to speak to our Father as well as listen to what He says. In fact, the Christian life begins with the Holy Spirit speaking in our hearts and giving us the assurance of salvation by saying, "Abba, Father" (Gal. 4:6), and we echo those words in our own witness (see Rom. 8:15). When the ascended Lord wanted to assure Ananias of Damascus that it was safe for him to go minister to Saul, He said to Ananias, "he is praying" (Acts 9:11). That was all the evidence Ananias needed.

Most of us don't understand the functioning of our own minds and bodies, and yet we're able to live somewhat normal lives in a difficult world. I can't explain the workings of my car and yet I can drive it, and even though the operating mechanisms of my computer completely baffle me, I can turn the computer on and off and write letters and books. I hear you saying, "But wait a minute. The better you understand both your car and your computer, the better you'll relate to them and use them." Agreed. *And the better I know the Lord and His Word, the better I'll be able to pray and see God answer.* But I don't have to wait until I have a Ph.D. in prayer to be able to come to the throne of grace. Even a baby Christian can cry, "Abba—Papa—Father!"

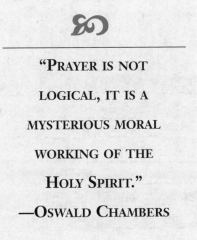

"PRAYER IS NOT LOGICAL, IT IS A MYSTERIOUS MORAL WORKING OF THE HOLY SPIRIT."
—OSWALD CHAMBERS

Someone asked Mrs. Albert Einstein, "Do you understand Dr. Einstein's mathematical equations?" She replied, "No, but I understand Dr. Einstein." Do I understand the eternal equations involved in praying to my Father? No, but I am getting to understand the Father better, and this helps me to pray.

Many of the Pharisees Jesus met knew their theology, but they didn't know God. The scribes counted the letters of the words written on their sacred Old Testament scrolls, but they overlooked learning about the God who wrote those words through His servants. Thirty years after his conversion, Paul prayed, "I want to know Christ" (Phil. 3:10)—and Paul had already been to heaven and back! Paul knew that knowing God better is the open secret of a successful Christian life, including a successful life of prayer. Certainly there's an important place for systematic theology in the Christian's curriculum, but only if it leads to a better knowledge of the Lord Himself.

Why, then, do we pray? Because prayer is God's ordained method for glorifying Himself by meeting our needs so that we can do His will and His work. "You do not have, because you do not ask God" (James 4:2). The same God who ordains the end also ordains the means to the end, and prayer is an important part of that means. When God wants to accomplish something, He raises up a man or a woman, or perhaps a group of believers, to pray about that very matter, and through their prayers He accomplishes His work.

It was God's plan that David become king of Israel and that from David's family the Redeemer would be born, so He raised up Hannah to pray for a son, and that son, Samuel, anointed David to be king.

God had a timetable for His people and ordained that they would be delivered from captivity after seventy years. When Daniel understood this promise, he immediately began to pray that the Lord would fulfill it, and God did (see Dan. 9).

It was God's will that the promised forerunner (see Isa. 40:1–5; Mal. 4:5–6) introduce the Redeemer to the nation of Israel. So, He moved Elizabeth and Zechariah to pray for a son, and John the Baptist was born. Before Jesus was born, godly people like Anna and Simeon were praying for the promised Messiah to come (see Luke 2:21–38), and God answered their prayers.

"Whether we like it or not," said Charles Spurgeon, "asking is the rule of the Kingdom." Asking humbles us, but it also glorifies God.

It hasn't been granted to us to understand fully the mysterious relationship between the eternal counsels of God, the promises of God, and the cries of His people, nor is it necessary that we understand. God is "over all and through all and in all" (Eph. 4:6), and His providence, power, and presence guarantee that His purposes will be accomplished. But in His grace, He has given us the privilege of prayer so that we might share in His great work of saving sinners and building His church. "We have not the remotest conception of what is done by our prayers," wrote Oswald Chambers, "nor have we the right to try and examine and understand it; all we know is that Jesus Christ laid all stress on prayer" (*Biblical Psychology*, p. 159). Godly Robert Murray M'Cheyne wrote, "If the veil of the world's machinery were lifted off, how much we would find is done in answer to the prayers of God's children."

If you need a definition of prayer, here's one to consider:

Prayer is the means God has ordained to glorify
Himself by sharing His love with His children, meeting
their needs, and accomplishing His purposes through

their lives and the lives of others.

This suggested definition covers some of the various aspects of prayer:

worship—glorifying God
communion—loving God
petition—asking God for what we need
intercession—asking God for what others need

A balanced Christian life begins with a balanced prayer life. Prayer is serious business, and it must be founded on the character and the promises of God. Unfortunately, we sometimes pick up unbiblical and ungodly ideas that influence our prayers and hinder the Lord from answering us. Unwittingly, we imitate the way others pray, and these ideas stick in our minds and take over. A. W. Tozer used to remind us, "The essence of idolatry is the entertainment of thoughts about God that are unworthy of Him" (*The Knowledge of the Holy*, p. 11). No professing Christian would deliberately bow before a pagan idol, but many of God's children ignorantly ask God to give and to do that which is completely contrary to His character and His written Word.

In the first section of this book, we will think together about some of these popular "routine religious statements" that are often used when God's children pray, and we will find out why they are dangerous. Before we can plant the seeds of prayer and cultivate healthy plants that bear fruit, we have to pull up a few of the weeds.

"HE DONE PRAYED MY HOT DOG COLD!"

႙

Here is a generic version of a story that was told to me by a man who was there (the details have been deleted so as to protect this author and the people who were involved):

At the annual conference of an evangelical mission board, while the ladies were at a fancy tea, the men and children gathered to enjoy an old-fashioned outdoor wiener roast. As we all know, at informal picnic gatherings protocol demands that somebody ask the blessing *before* the guests visit the tables and fill their plates. But on this occasion, the leader had the picnickers get their food first, and then he asked the guest speaker to pray. The good man prayed his way up and down the Himalayas and around the equator, and when he finally said, "Amen," everybody heard a young boy say very loudly to his father, "Daddy, he done prayed my hot dog cold!"

In a similar vein, I heard the story of an Air Force cadet who wasn't ashamed of his faith, so at meals he would reverently bow his head, close his eyes, and pray silently for several minutes. One day while he was praying, somebody stole his plate and hid it. Did he ever get it back? I hope so, but I really don't know. If he did, he had probably prayed his rations cold.

As Paul wrote in Galatians 4:24, these figurative illustrations "are an allegory" (KJV), so let's try to garner from them some truths to help us in our own prayer life.

ॐ

To begin with, *why do we pray before we eat?* I once asked a group of college students that question, and they roared with laughter. One of them said, "If you saw the food we're served in the dining room, you'd pray too!" (I don't think that's true anymore. I've eaten excellent meals in college dining rooms.) In another instance, I remember a missionary leader who sometimes ended his table prayer with "And, Lord, kill the bugs." Well, he knew the situation better than we did. But back to our question: "Why do we pray before we eat?"

Obviously, we're giving thanks to the Lord for the food He's provided for us. We're grateful to God. Jesus taught us to pray for daily bread, and when the bread is before us, we want to be thankful for God's gifts and for His faithfulness in caring for us. Before Jesus fed the 5,000, He looked up to heaven and prayed (see Mark 6:41), and He also gave thanks at the Last Supper (see Mark 14:22; 1 Cor. 11:24). Paul gave thanks for his food while he was on board a ship during a storm, and it encouraged the passengers and crew to eat and to trust God (see Acts 27:35–36).

First Timothy 4:1–5 warns us not to follow false teachers who ignore what Jesus taught in Mark 7 and what the early church decided in Acts 15, that all foods are clean and should be received with thanksgiving. That's what Paul meant when he wrote, "[I]t [the food] is consecrated by the word of God and prayer" (1 Tim. 4:5). The Scriptures say that the food is "clean" and prayer consecrates the food to the Lord so that He can use it to sustain us. (That doesn't mean that all foods are good for all of us. If you're diabetic, as I am, it will take more than the Word and prayer to make a big piece of key lime pie "clean" for us!)

My heritage is Swedish and German, and very early on I learned that my Scandinavian relatives also gave thanks *after* the meal. After enjoying coffee, homemade cake, and bilingual conversation, my Uncle Simon Carlson would bow his head and give thanks in Swedish, and that was the signal that the meal had ended. As a child, I thought this was a strange practice, until years later when I read Deuteronomy 8:10: "When you have eaten and are satisfied, praise the LORD your God for the good land he has given you." Thanking God after the meal is an excellent discipline for people who are prone to eat too much during the meal, for how can they sincerely give thanks for those extra pounds they just put on? (I'm writing myself under conviction.)

It appears, then, that a table prayer is first of all an expression of thanks to the Lord for His gracious provision. It's also a consecration of the food *and of ourselves as God's children, who are strengthened by the food so that we may serve and glorify God.* If God provides food for my body and wants to be glorified in and through my body, then not to thank Him for food is base ingratitude. So is enjoying that food and then using my body in any way I please. A table prayer ought to be much more than a religious ritual. As we join our hearts with the one who is leading us in prayer, we should make it a time of both gratitude and dedication to the Lord.

$$\mathcal{EO}$$

So, then, how long should a table prayer be? Answer: Long enough to accomplish the above two purposes.

But what if the Spirit leads us to pray longer? Answer: "The spirits of prophets are subject to the control of prophets" (1 Cor. 14:32). If that's true of people who preach, would it not also be true of people who pray? After all, if the preacher or the pray-er really is Spirit filled, he or she will produce the fruit of the Spirit, which includes *self-control.* People who lose control aren't filled

> $\mathcal{EO}$
>
> THE LORD SOMETIMES TELLS PEOPLE TO STOP PRAYING.

with the Spirit; they're fooled by other spirits and following the flesh.

More than once in my conference ministry, I've experienced the truth of John 10:8: "All who ... came before me were thieves and robbers." The speakers who went before me took more time than was allotted to them, and I was left with very little time for presenting the message I'd prepared. After the meeting, these speakers would excuse their thievery by saying, "You know, when the Spirit's in control, you just have to keep going." But the Spirit was not in control, or they would have exercised self-control and watched the clock. Many years of radio ministry have taught me to say what I have to say right the first time and not waste expensive radio minutes circling the field and looking for a place to land. What applies to preaching should also apply to prayer.

Evangelist George Whitfield said of a certain preacher, "He prayed me into a good frame of mind, and if he had stopped there, it would have been very well; but he prayed me out of it again by keeping on." During one of his evangelistic campaigns, Dwight L. Moody asked a minister to lead in prayer, and the man went on and on and on, and people began to leave the hall. Moody finally said, "While our brother is finishing his prayer, we shall sing a hymn." Moody didn't want the well-meaning preacher to pray the meeting cold. And didn't Jesus have something to say about people who try to impress us with long prayers (see Matt. 23:14 KJV)?

෨

It surprises some people to learn that _the Lord sometimes tells_ _people to stop praying._ When Israel came to the Red Sea after their exodus from Egypt, Moses was silently crying out to God for help as he tried to still the people. The Lord knew this and said to him, "Why are you crying out to me? Tell the Israelites to move on" (Ex. 14:15). Stop praying and get moving! (More than one church needs to hear that command.)

After the Lord told Moses he was not allowed to enter Canaan (see Num. 20:1–13), Moses prayed for God to remove that discipline and let him go into the land. (I get the impression that Moses prayed this prayer frequently.) One day the Lord told Moses to drop the matter from his prayer list, and he obeyed (see Deut. 3:23–39).

After the humiliating defeat of Israel at Ai (see Josh. 7), Joshua tore his clothes, fell on his face, and spent all day crying out to God. God's response was, "Stand up! What are you doing down on your face?" (Josh. 7:10). There was a traitor in the camp, and God expected Joshua to help expose him.

After Paul had prayed three times for healing, the Lord graciously stopped him and promised to give him grace to turn his burden into a blessing.

In my own prayer experience, several times I've been praying about some matter only to have the Lord convince me after a few weeks that it was time to stop. The request was either out of His will or the answer was on its way. I didn't know then which it was, but I obediently stopped praying and later found out the result. Sometimes the red light flashes from a statement in the Bible. On other occasions, the signal is just a conviction in my heart, given, I trust, by the Holy Spirit.

Yes, there's a time to pray, but there's also a time to act, for the Lord wants us to be a part of the answer to our prayers. I'll say more about this when we get to Part IV and take inventory of our prayers.

ઈ

Let's hear the conclusion of the matter. If you are called to give God thanks for a meal, simply ask Him to bless the gifts and the recipients. Stick to that agenda and don't go on detours. If you have special burdens on your heart and feel led to share them, perhaps you could do so after the meal and request that someone pray with you. If the other diners aren't in a hurry, you might remain at the table for a brief prayer meeting after the meal.

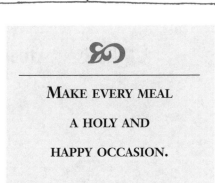

MAKE EVERY MEAL A HOLY AND HAPPY OCCASION.

I'm sure that God can bless a cold hot dog, but why expect Him to do it? For that matter, God can perform a miracle and keep a hot dog warm while somebody's praying at length, but He never wastes miracles. Expecting that approach is very near to tempting God.

Make every meal a holy and happy occasion. Remember what Moses and the elders experienced on Mt. Sinai: "they saw God, and they ate and drank" (Ex. 24:11). The experience of the two Emmaus disciples was similar. Jesus gave thanks and broke the bread and "their eyes were opened and they recognized him" (Luke 24:31).

To quote Spurgeon again, "When you pray in public, as a rule, the shorter the better" (*Metropolitan Tabernacle Pulpit*, vol. 15, p. 106).

3

"I HAVE AN UNSPEAKABLE REQUEST"

ॐ

The person who made this statement probably meant to say, "I have an *unspoken* request," although the prayer burden may have been so great that it couldn't be easily expressed. Asaph, the temple musician, recorded that kind of an experience in Psalm 77:4: "I was too troubled to speak." And, once, David tried to stay silent but couldn't—his heart grew hot within him, "the fire burned," and he had to open his mouth and say what was on his heart, come what may (see Ps. 39:1–3). However, if saying "unspeakable" instead of "unspoken" was a slip of the tongue, I suspect it was a "Freudian slip" that revealed what was really in the person's heart. The request was something so terrible that it had to stay buried.

This brings up the whole subject of "unspoken prayer requests."

I had never heard anyone say, "I have an unspoken request," until I began to minister in the Southland, where I discovered that it was a common practice. I recall being in one church where the pastor announced, "A radio listener

24

has phoned asking us to remember forty-seven unspoken requests." At the time, I was puzzled as to how the church would intercede for this believer, because I didn't know how *I* would pray for forty-seven unknown needs. It would take less time to pray for the forty-seven requests collectively than individually—"Lord, help this radio listener with these many burdens and show her what you want her to do"—but is this effective praying?

Of course, we know why some people don't want to state their prayer burdens openly: their concerns are too personal, painful, and embarrassing. (But forty-seven of them?) If a request involves another person, speaking about it publicly might make the problem worse. For example, a mother tells her prayer group that her child is about to be thrown out of college, somebody repeats it, and the word begins to spread (of course, with the qualification of "I'm not gossiping, you understand. I just want to share this prayer burden with you"). Nevertheless, the child hears about it and declares war on his mother and the prayer group. To tell an entire congregation about an abusive husband or a wayward relative may turn out to be both a declaration of faith and a declaration of war.

But if I can pray for a friend's forty-seven unspoken requests all at once, why can't I share forty-seven *spoken* requests of my own all at once and save even more time? "Lord, here is my prayer list. You see it. Meet these forty-seven needs." I've searched the Bible and can find no examples of believers sharing unspoken requests, nor can I find any instructions for handling such requests. Hannah didn't tell Eli what her burden was, but neither did she call her burden an "unspoken request." At first Eli misunderstood her and scolded her, but then he realized that she was sincere and was seeking God's help (see 1 Sam. 1:9–18).

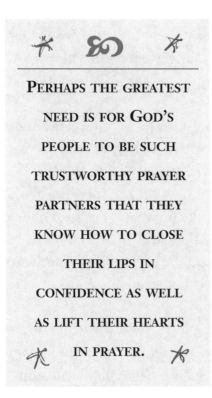

> PERHAPS THE GREATEST NEED IS FOR GOD'S PEOPLE TO BE SUCH TRUSTWORTHY PRAYER PARTNERS THAT THEY KNOW HOW TO CLOSE THEIR LIPS IN CONFIDENCE AS WELL AS LIFT THEIR HEARTS IN PRAYER.

Nehemiah's burden for Jerusalem was so great that even the pagan king saw the evidence of it on his face and asked what was wrong. Nehemiah then told the king his concern, requested official help, and the Lord answered his prayers (see Neh. 2:1–9). The household of Chloe didn't write to Paul, "We have ten unspoken requests involving the church here in Corinth." Instead, they sent him a detailed letter describing the church's problems and asking him to answer their questions (see 1 Cor. 1:11). Did this make Chloe's household more popular among the carnal Christians in the church? Probably not, but the Lord used that letter to produce Paul's inspired response, and his letter helped the Corinthian church and has helped believers ever since.

We will not solve the "unspoken request" problem by refusing to consider such prayer burdens but by encouraging people to be as specific as they can without breaking confidence. "I have four unspoken requests" might stir up more effective prayer support if it was phrased, "I have four critical decisions to make, and I need wisdom," or "There are four problem people in my life, and I need God's help in facing and handling them." But perhaps the greatest need is for God's people to be such trustworthy prayer partners that they know how to close their lips in confidence as well as lift their hearts in prayer. How I thank the Lord for believers who have prayed with me about critical matters and didn't announce the details at the next prayer meeting they attended.

If you're a believer who has a secret battle to fight or a heavy burden to bear and you don't want to advertise it, rest on what God says in Romans 8:26–27: Your heavenly Father understands "unspoken requests" (and even "unspeakable requests"), and He encourages you to come boldly ("with freedom of speech") to the throne of grace. Also, ask Him to provide a confidential prayer partner with whom you can share your burdens and whose burdens you can share. After all, "two are better than one" (see Eccl. 4:9–12).

4

"Lord, May This Accident Not Have Happened!"

૭૭

That request was sent heavenward by a young man who had wrecked his father's car, but the evidence in the police files did not indicate that his petition was answered.

The boy's "prayer" reminds me of Ambrose Bierce's famous definition of prayer: "Asking that the laws of the universe be annulled on behalf of a single petitioner, confessedly unworthy." This definition produces a smile and aptly describes the boy's prayer (and perhaps some of *our* prayers), but Bierce's definition is as foolish as the prayer.

Granted, in answer to prayer, God has been known to suspend the laws He built into His universe so that He might accomplish His great purposes. He did it for Moses at the Red Sea, for Joshua at the Jordan River, and for Jesus when He healed the afflicted and raised the dead—and when Jesus Himself was raised from the dead. Of course, the greatest miracle God ever performs in response to prayer is the forgiveness of our sins and the transformation of our lives as we walk with Him. That will last for eternity.

So God could have answered this young man's prayer. All He had to do was reverse the spin of the earth so that time went backward to a point before the accident occurred and then prevent the accident. Or He might have spoken the word and restored both the boy and the vehicle to their pre-accident conditions. "Is anything too hard for the LORD?" (Gen. 18:14). But if the Lord prevented or reversed the consequences of every foolish thing we did in violation of His will, we would never build character or become trustworthy servants who sincerely want to do His will. If God operated as the teenager wanted Him to, we wouldn't have to worry about disobedience or folly. If we did a dumb thing, God would just kiss it and make it well, and we would never learn from our mistakes. But it doesn't work that way (thankfully).

GOD HAS BEEN KNOWN TO SUSPEND THE LAWS HE BUILT INTO HIS UNIVERSE SO THAT HE MIGHT ACCOMPLISH HIS GREAT PURPOSES.

"Lord, may this accident not have happened" is not really a prayer; it's an expression of juvenile religious wishful thinking. Like Adam and Eve, the young man believed the Devil's lie, "You will not surely die" (Gen. 3:4). In other words, "There are no consequences to foolishness and disobedience!" But the boy's prayer, foolish as it is, touches on a subject that is vital to a successful prayer life, and that's the relationship between prayer and the sovereignty of God.

જી

After his restoration to sanity—and probably his conversion to faith in the God of Israel—King Nebuchadnezzar
uttered a powerful statement of his faith in the sovereignty
of God.

> His dominion is an eternal dominion;
> his kingdom endures from generation
> to generation.
> All the peoples of the earth
> are regarded as nothing.
> He does as he pleases
> with the powers of heaven
> and the peoples of the earth.
> No one can hold back his hand
> or say to him, "What have you done?"
> (Dan. 4:34–35)

That's the kind of God we worship and serve, the kind
of God to whom we pray! Ignore the sovereignty of God
and you not only silence worship and prayer, but you foolishly abandon the very source of life, wisdom, and
strength. After Peter and John were released by the author-
ities and warned not to preach again in the name of Jesus,
they didn't stage a protest or seek political protection. *They
went to a church prayer meeting and prayed to Almighty God!*
This is how they prayed:

"Sovereign Lord," they said, "you made the heaven and the earth and the sea, and everything in them. You spoke by the Holy Spirit through the mouth of your servant, our father David:

"'Why do the nations rage
and the peoples plot in vain?
The kings of the earth take their stand
and the rulers gather together against
the Lord and against his Anointed One.'

Indeed, Herod and Pontius Pilate met together with the Gentiles and the people of Israel in this city to conspire against your holy servant Jesus, whom you anointed. They did what your power and will had decided beforehand should happen. Now, Lord, consider their threats and enable your servants to speak your word with great boldness. Stretch out your hand to heal and perform miraculous signs and wonders through the name of your holy servant Jesus."

After they prayed, the place where they were meeting was shaken. And they were all filled with the Holy Spirit and spoke the word of God boldly. (Acts 4:24–31)

The record of this event makes it clear that there is no conflict between the sovereignty of God and the believing prayers of His people. The same God who ordains the end also ordains the means-to-the-end prayer in the name of Jesus. The God to whom they prayed is "sovereign Lord"—literally, "despot"— and His sovereignty is seen in the fact that He created the heavens and the earth. Jesus called Him "Lord of heaven and earth" (Luke 10:21), and Paul said that Jesus today is "far above all rule and authority, power and dominion, and every title that can be given" (Eph. 1:21). It seems incredible, but when we pray to the Lord in His will, we are privileged to lay hold of the almighty power that created and sustains the universe.

> **IF WE ARE FILLED WITH GOD'S SPIRIT AND GOD'S WORD, THEN HIS DESIRES WILL BE OUR DESIRES, AND WE WILL PRAY IN HIS WILL.**

The prayer of Peter and John was based on God's Word, specifically Psalm 2, for the Word of God and prayer must always go together. "If you remain in me and my words remain in you," said Jesus; "ask whatever you wish, and it will be given you" (John 15:7). If we are filled with God's Spirit (see Eph. 5:18) and God's Word (see Col. 3:16), then His desires will be our desires, and we will pray in His will. Archbishop Trench said, "Praying is not overcoming God's reluctance; it is laying hold of His highest willingness." And Robert Law, in his commentary on 1 John, *The Tests of Life*, wrote, "Prayer is a mighty instrument, not for getting man's will done in heaven, but for getting God's will done on earth" (p. 304).

The challenging thing about this prayer of the early church is that it wasn't directed *against* their opponents. The believers didn't ask the Lord to stop the persecution (the persecution actually grew worse) or to destroy the enemies of the gospel. They asked the Lord to give the church power to witness with boldness so that they would glorify the name of Jesus (see Acts 4:29–30). The focus was not on their comfort or even their safety but on the glory of the sovereign God. "Do not pray for easy lives," said Phillips Brooks. "Pray to be better men and women. Do not pray for tasks equal to your powers; pray for powers equal to your tasks."

A Christian, angry at what he considered government interference in his life, prayed publicly that God "would kill or convert every elected state official." The request for their salvation was biblical, but the request for their death was not. If anybody had a right to pray God's judgment on their persecutors and murderers it was Jesus and Stephen, yet both of them prayed that their murderers would be forgiven (see Luke 23:34; Acts 7:60).

The early church prayed "enable your servants" (Acts 4:29), and God answered their prayer. He shook the place where they were meeting and filled the believers with His Spirit, and in spite of the official order to keep quiet, they spoke the word of God boldly. "The place was shaken," said Chrysostom, "and that made them all the more unshaken" (*The Nicene and Post-Nicene Fathers*, vol. 11, p. 73).

ॐ

As I think about the relationship between prayer and the sovereignty of God, the prayer of Abraham in Genesis 18:22–33 comes to mind. The Lord told Abraham that He was planning to destroy Sodom, and Abraham was concerned because his nephew Lot lived there with his family. Furthermore, Abraham didn't want the people of Sodom—people he had once rescued (see Gen. 14)—to perish, ungodly as they were. Abraham had a burden for his lost neighbors and interceded for them.

God revealed His plan to Abraham because He had chosen him as His servant, so we have here the sovereign grace of God. But in doing this, the Lord was giving Abraham opportunity to respond. Deeply hurt by his nephew's lack of spiritual discernment, Abraham might have said, "Lot got himself into this mess, so let him suffer. And as for the people of Sodom, they're so wicked they ought to be judged!"

But he didn't respond with self-righteous anger; instead, he "approached" the Lord with his prayer. The Hebrew word means not only "to draw near" but also "to argue a case in court" (see Isa. 41:1, 21). Abraham asked the Lord to spare the wicked city of Sodom for the sake of the righteous people living there, meaning Lot and his family (see 2 Peter 2:6–8). It appears that Lot and his wife had at least two married daughters and two single daughters. If Lot had won to the Lord his wife, his single daughters, his married daughters and their husbands, *and two other people,* the whole city would have been spared. As it was, the people of Sodom went into eternity without God.

Abraham's appeal was based on the justice of God. He wasn't arguing or bargaining with God or trying to change God's sovereign will. If God had said no, Abraham would have stopped interceding. But, though Lot should not have been living in Sodom, it would be wrong for the Lord to treat him the same way He treated Lot's wicked neighbors. There's no evidence that Lot lived *like* the people in Sodom; he only lived *among* them. So Abraham humbled himself before the Lord and sought to convince Him to spare the city. Godly Samuel Rutherford wrote, "It is faith's work to claim and challenge loving-kindnesses out of all the roughest strokes of God." That's what Abraham was doing.

The two angels didn't find ten righteous people in the city, but they did offer Lot's family a gracious opportunity to escape. The married daughters remained in Sodom with their husbands, but Lot made his escape with his wife and two single daughters. His wife disobeyed God and looked back at Sodom as they left, and she was instantly judged. In the end, God saved Lot and his two daughters for the sake of Abraham. Let's keep in mind that God saves sinners today, not because they deserve it, but for the sake of His Son.

৯৩

If your views of the sovereignty of God keep you from witnessing or praying, then those views are incorrect. In His sovereign grace, our God is calling out a people for His name so that we can witness and preach with confidence, knowing that His Word will not be wasted. God is in complete control of the universe, so we can pray to Him without fear. We don't always know what to pray for or how to preach the Word, but if our faith is in God almighty, Maker of heaven and earth (see Ps. 124:8), and if our desire is "Hallowed be your name" (Matt. 6:9), then our sovereign Lord will hear and work according to His will.

We should never boast about answers to prayer, because these gifts are all from God. Nor should we despair over unanswered prayer or answers that are different from what we prayed for, because our loving Father knows what is best. "In all our praying, however," wrote A. W. Tozer, "it is important that we keep in mind that God will not alter His eternal purposes at the word of a man. We do not pray in order to persuade God to change His mind.... What the praying man does is to bring his will into line with the will of God so God can do what He has all along been willing to do" (*The Price of Neglect*, pp. 51–52). After all, don't we pray, "Your will be done on earth as it is in heaven" (Matt. 6:10)? One of God's most painful disciplines is to give His children what they want when He has something better in store. Many of us have lived long enough to be thankful for *unanswered* prayer.

So, if you wreck the car and find yourself in a really tough situation, don't ask the Lord, "*How* can I get out of this?" but "What can I get out of this? *What* is your will?" God reversed the shadow on the sundial for Hezekiah (see Isa. 38:7–8) and delayed the sunset for Joshua (see Josh. 10:12–15), and He can still do such miracles today. But we must remember to pray as Jesus did: "My Father, if it is possible, may this cup be taken from me. Yet not as I will, but as you will" (Matt. 26:39). God still gives His best to those who leave the choice with Him.

5

"Let's Have a Word of Prayer"

ॐ

Truth be told, it would probably be better just to say, "Let's pray." Or perhaps, "Let's invest some time in prayer."

After all, what is "a word of prayer"? According to the dictionary, to have "a word" with somebody means to engage in a very short conversation. But I've heard people say, "Let's have a word of prayer" and then proceed to pray for ten minutes.

Alas, these evangelical clichés get stuck in our brains, and we use them routinely without realizing what we're doing! It's all part of the fixtures of a traditional prayer meeting, but when our prayer meetings become traditional, we'd better start praying for revival. Every time we say, "Let's have a word of prayer," we may be giving evidence that we're not really thinking about the seriousness of prayer. In fact, sometimes our words just run together:

"Let'shaveawordofprayerOurFatherinheaven ..."

and off we go.

But we know that rushing into God's presence like this is not the way God wants us to pray. To be sure, in emergency situations—as when Peter started sinking in the Sea of Galilee—we don't have time to prepare ourselves to pray and can only cry out, "Lord, save me!" But unless you're a race car driver or a wild animal trainer, those dangerous occasions are probably not that frequent in your life.

When I was serving with Youth for Christ (YFC)

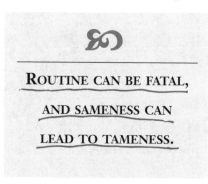

ROUTINE CAN BE FATAL, AND SAMENESS CAN LEAD TO TAMENESS.

International, I quickly learned the importance of prayer, because YFC operated from one miracle to another. We met in regular prayer meetings, as well as in spontaneous ones as needs arose, and at these gatherings Bob Cook and Ted Engstrom used to remind us to "get rid of our routine prayers" so that we could get down to business and really pray.

I discovered that "routine praying" was a problem in my own prayer life. How easy it is to put the "prayer CD" in the slot, push the start button, and recite to the Lord the same requests in the same order day after day. This practice might be included in what Jesus called "babbling like pagans" (Matt. 6:7; "vain repetitions" in the KJV), a phrase that my Greek lexicon translates as "speaking without thinking." This can be a problem, especially for people who have a list of items that they pray about every day.

Keeping prayer fresh and vibrant is the result of worshipping the Lord, feeding joyfully on the Word, yielding to the Spirit, focusing on what we think and say, and not allowing the "weariness of the flesh" to take over. If you're in a group prayer meeting, pay close attention to what the other people pray about. If you're the leader, be sure the atmosphere stays fresh (remember Eutychus? See Acts 20:7–12), and encourage the participants occasionally to stand, sing, and gather in small groups. Routine can be fatal, and sameness can lead to tameness. It's helpful to write the prayer requests on a blackboard (or whiteboard) that everybody can see, and printed prayer lists are useful in the meeting and can be taken home.

One word of caution: As we seek to eliminate the clichés from our praying, let's be careful not to become "cute." Prayer is not the vehicle for displaying our vocabulary, our cleverness, or the verses we've memorized. "Do not be quick with your mouth," warned Solomon. "Do not be hasty in your heart to utter anything before God" (Eccl. 5:2). If we're faithful in our private prayers and honest with God, we'll have no problem carrying that sincerity into a public prayer meeting. Paul exhorted us to "pray continually" (1 Thess. 5:17), not just to "have a word of prayer."

"Thank You, Father, for Dying for Us on the Cross"

ഔ

I actually heard a church staff person use those words in the opening prayer of a morning worship service. Obviously he wasn't prepared to pray and probably had been drafted at the last minute. I've been in worship services where the pastoral prayers were on TV monitors facing the pulpit, and all the pastor had to do was read them with sincere feeling. While that might seem to some to lack the supposed authenticity of spontaneity, it's better than hasty prayers that confuse the persons of the Godhead and promote other doctrinal aberrations.

Charles Spurgeon once told his ministerial students to follow his example and prepare their pulpit prayers, by which he meant thinking them through (not necessarily writing them out). If we prepare our messages and make outlines to guide us, why not prepare our prayers as well? At least then we can focus on the Lord and remember that when we pray we say, "Our Father …"

"We'll Just Have to Pray for Good Luck"

෨

I don't remember the context in which I heard this statement, but I do remember how shocked I was to hear someone link prayer and luck in the same sentence. It's obvious that if we live by prayer, then we believe in God and trust His wise providence. If we live by luck, then we believe in a world of chance over which nobody has any control. It's depressing to see people read their horoscopes, consult tarot cards, pay gurus to channel a "spirit," and even phone television spiritualists for help, totally ignorant of the fact that none of these activities will enable them to understand or control the future.

I've noticed that people who mingle faith in God with faith in luck usually blame bad luck when they fail but rarely thank God when they succeed. If someone they don't like succeeds, the reason is good luck and not hard work. If they themselves succeed, it was due to hard work, not the blessing of God. None of these people has the testimony of Abraham's devoted servant: "As for me, the Lord has led me on the journey" (Gen. 24:27).

Jacob's unwanted wife Leah may have had a trace of this

kind of superstition in her genetic structure. She shared her
maid Zilpah with Jacob and then gave the name "Gad" to the
first son who was born to Zilpah (see Gen. 30:9–10). Gad
means "fortune" and was the name of a pagan god. Consider
God's response to the matter:

> "But as for you who forsake the LORD
> and forget my holy mountain,
> who spread a table for Fortune [*gad*]
> and fill bowls of mixed wine for Destiny [*meni*],
> I will destine you for the sword" (Isa. 65:11–12).

Devout Jews put no confidence in such things as luck and
chance because they believed that God Almighty was in control of the universe, and that included their personal lives and
the future of their nation (see Gen. 28:15; Ps. 34:20). From
the human point of view it sometimes appeared that "time
and chance" were determining events (see Eccl. 9:11), but
the Jews knew that Jehovah was on the throne.

"The lot is cast into the lap, but its every decision is from
the LORD" (Prov. 16:33). It looked like luck that Ruth went to
glean in the fields of Boaz, but this decision was an act of
God's providence. Even bitter Naomi recognized the hand of
God in the event (see Ruth 2:19–23). The movement of the
donkeys in 1 Samuel 9 wasn't chance, it was providence; and
David's frequent narrow escapes from King Saul were the
result of heaven's care more than David's strategy: "My help
comes from the LORD, the Maker of heaven and earth" (Ps.
121:2). New Testament Christians had the same kind of faith
(see Acts 4:27–30; Rom. 8:28), and so should we.

8

"Whisper a Prayer for Me"

&

The popular television host Bill Moyers served on the White House staff when Lyndon B. Johnson was president. An ordained minister, Moyers was often asked by the president to offer thanks at staff meals. While Moyers was praying at one luncheon, the president said, "Speak up, I can't hear you!" to which Moyers responded, "I'm not talking to you."

It's not likely that President Johnson thought he was God and *had* to hear the prayer but only that he was at the table and *wanted* to hear the prayer and participate in the act of blessing. I find myself sympathizing with the president, for I've sat at many tables and also conducted many prayer meetings in which I've been perplexed by people who have prayed quietly to themselves, making it impossible for us to pray with them or even say a quiet "Amen!" to a request.

Another story of an opposite sort of problem also comes to mind. One of the greatest prayer warriors I ever knew was Peter Deyneka Sr., founder of the Slavic Gospel Association.

When I was pastoring in Chicago, Peter and I often met for prayer, and the experience was a rich one. At an all-night Youth for Christ prayer meeting in the Westminster Hotel at Winona Lake, Indiana, Peter was praying fervently, and his volume was increasing with each request. One of the guests in the hotel, who was trying to sleep, became disturbed by Peter's voice and sent a note down asking that we lower the decibels. One of the men said, "Peter, God isn't deaf," to which Peter replied, "He isn't nervous, either" and went right on praying.

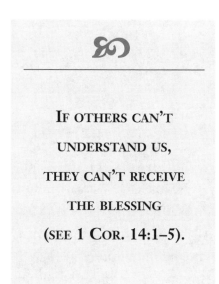

IF OTHERS CAN'T UNDERSTAND US, THEY CAN'T RECEIVE THE BLESSING (SEE 1 COR. 14:1–5).

Perhaps we should pray somewhere between these two extremes. Yes, prayer is an intimate conversation with God, but when others are praying with us, let's not act as though God pays attention only to us. We have every right to pray silently in our hearts as Hannah did (see 1 Sam. 1:9–18), but if we are praying publicly with a group, let's speak up so they can hear and pray with us. What Paul wrote about tongues could be applied to public prayer: If others can't understand us, they can't receive the blessing (see 1 Cor. 14:1–5). This doesn't mean that in our prayers we speak to others over the Lord's shoulder, although I've heard that kind of praying ("Lord, help our pastor be well prepared next Lord's Day"). It simply means that we strengthen the fellowship by praying so that others can hear us and share the burdens with us.

When I was a lad in Sunday school, we occasionally sang a little chorus that I haven't heard in decades:

> Whisper a prayer in the morning,
> Whisper a prayer at noon,
> Whisper a prayer in the evening,
> To keep your heart in tune.

Praying in the morning, at noon, and in the evening is biblical, and I highly recommend it. Daniel did it (see Dan. 6:10), and so did David (see Ps. 55:17). But why must we whisper? If we're alone, we can speak to God out loud, and if we're with strangers on a bus or in a doctor's waiting room, we can pray in our hearts and He will hear us. Unlike the Pharisees, we don't want to demonstrate on the street corners our prowess in prayer (see Matt. 6:5), but neither do we want to imitate the mediums and spiritists "who whisper and mutter" (Isa. 8:19). The people mentioned in Isaiah 26:16 were too weak to call, so they whispered.

When D. L. Moody was ministering in Great Britain in 1873, the popular magazine *The Christian* published his suggestions for leading a successful prayer meeting. Moody sent copies to all the Protestant ministers in the British Isles, and they greatly appreciated it. Here's a summary of what he wrote:

> Get the people sitting close together; ventilate the meeting place; keep the singing lively; let the prayers

be specific and the minister brief in his remarks; announce the subjects in advance; don't scold those who come for those who don't; keep your discouragement to yourself and God; vary hymns with prayers, so that not more than two prayers are consecutive; keep remarks informal, pointed, and the meeting short; get all to participate, even if you have to speak to them in private beforehand; avoid controversy; be punctual; and most important, keep in the Spirit (*They Called Him Mr. Moody* by Richard K. Curtis, p. 181).

I would add one more suggestion: Encourage people to speak up when they pray so that all may participate.

9

"Don't Wrestle in Prayer— Just Believe"

$$\mathscr{E}$$

My dear friend Dr. Howard Sugden and I were two of the three speakers at a summer Bible conference at which the third speaker was rather unhappy with us. Perhaps he felt threatened by Dr. Sugden's stature and popularity as a preacher, or maybe he was just having a bad week. We all have them. At any rate, he decided one day to challenge a statement one of us had made in a message about "wrestling in prayer."

"Prayer isn't a wrestling match with God," he said with great intensity. "Prayer is a beautiful conversation with God. We believe, we ask, and He gives."

Dr. Sugden and I said nothing, but I'm sure he was recalling Colossians 4:12 just as I was.

> Epaphras, who is one of you and a servant of
> Christ Jesus, sends greetings. He is always wrestling
> in prayer for you, that you may stand firm in all the
> will of God, mature and fully assured.

7

The Greek word translated "wrestling" is *agonizomai* and gives us the English word *agonize*. Instead of having a quiet and beautiful conversation with God, Epaphras was praying like a wrestler or a runner in the Olympic games, striving to win a gold medal. Paul also prayed this way. He asked his friends in Rome to join him in his "struggle [*sunagonizomai*] by praying to God" for him (Rom. 15:30). There are times when we need the endurance and determination of an athlete if our praying is going to accomplish the will of God.

This isn't to say that our personal pains and exertions will bend God's will, but neither does it suggest that it's a mark of deep spirituality to be cold and passive as we intercede for others. Jonathan Edwards wrote of David Brainerd,

> His life shows the right way to success in the works of the ministry. He sought it as a resolute soldier seeks victory in a siege or battle; or as a man that runs a race for a great prize. Animated with love to Christ and souls, how did he labor always fervently, not only in word and doctrine, in public and private, but in *prayers* day and night, "wrestling with God" in secret, and "travailing in birth," with unutterable groans and agonies.… [L]ike a true son of Jacob, he persevered in wrestling through all the darkness of the night, until the breaking of the day.

Charles Spurgeon quoted these words to his students in his lecture "The Preacher's Private Prayer," which was given at his pastors' college, but the quotation applies to every

Christian and not to ministers only. (I recommend the lecture to all believers.) Although careful exegetes correctly point out that Jacob's wrestling with the Lord recorded in Genesis 32:22–31 was not a prayer meeting as such but a battle of wills, it would be wonderful if in our own praying we imitated Jacob's determination and said, "I will not let you go unless you bless me" (Gen. 32:26).

> **IT WOULD BE WONDERFUL IF IN OUR OWN PRAYING WE IMITATED JACOB'S DETERMINATION AND SAID, "I WILL NOT LET YOU GO UNLESS YOU BLESS ME" (GEN. 32:26).**

If you need more evidence that prayer can involve wrestling, I put before you the example of our Lord Jesus Christ: "During the days of Jesus' life on earth, he offered up prayers and petitions with loud cries and tears to the one who could save him from death, and he was heard because of his reverent submission" (Heb. 5:7).

Like any metaphor, the phrase "wrestling with God" must be seen with the eyes of the heart. That blessed proponent of prayer E. M. Bounds puts it this way:

> Prayer in its highest and most availing form is
> accomplished with the attitude of wrestling with God.
> It is the contest and victory of faith, a victory not
> secured from an enemy but from one who tries our

> faith that he may enlarge and increase its desires.... The Bible is inexhaustible in its illustrations of the fact that the highest spiritual good is secured from the highest form of spiritual effort. Grace it is, but grace in its rewarding, compensating form. There is no room in the plans of grace for feeble desires, listless efforts, lazy attitudes. All must be ardent, vigorous, vigilant (*Prayer and Revival*, pp. 47–48).

Of course, the energy for "wrestling in prayer" must come from the Holy Spirit. "If the prayer originates with the Holy Spirit, then the wrestling can be beautiful and wonderful," wrote A. W. Tozer, "but if we are the victims of our own overheated desires, our praying can be as carnal as any other act" (*This World: Playground or Battleground?* p. 16). It's dangerous to bring false fire to the altar of the Lord. That's what killed Nadab and Abihu (see Lev. 10).

The tenth stanza of Charles Wesley's poem "Wrestling Jacob" says it well:

> My prayer hath power with God; the grace
> Unspeakable I now receive,
> Through faith I see thee face to face,
> I see thee face to face, and live;
> In vain I have not wept, and strove,
> Thy nature and thy name is Love.

The many images of prayer in Scripture remind us that our experiences at the throne of grace will vary from time to time, and this is a good thing. In the Jewish sanctuary, prayer was symbolized by the burning of incense on the golden altar before the veil (see Luke 1:8–9; Rev. 5:8). David in the wilderness couldn't visit the sanctuary, so he asked God to accept the lifting up of his hands to heaven as the equivalent of the burning incense (see Ps. 141:1–2; 1 Tim. 2:8). Daniel opened his windows toward Jerusalem when he prayed (see Dan. 6:10; 1 Kings 8:46–51), and Jesus instructed His disciples to close the door when they prayed (see Matt. 6:5–6). Abraham conversed with the Lord as he shared his burden (see Gen. 18:16–33), but King Hezekiah turned his face to the wall and fervently asked God to let him live (see Isa. 38:1–3). An angel had to strengthen Jesus in the garden, for He was in anguish, and "his sweat was like drops of blood falling to the ground" (Luke 22:44).

Whatever our posture or practices in prayer, so long as they aren't unbiblical, let's be sure we have passion in our prayers. "The earnest prayer of a righteous person has great power and wonderful results" (James 5:16 NLT). Quoting E. M. Bounds again, "Prayer, to be efficient, must have life. It must be living. It must be energized by all the forces that can be kindled in the soul by a great faith, a great need, and a great desire" (op. cit. p. 49).

If the Holy Spirit is assisting us in our praying "with groans that words cannot express" (Rom. 8:26), then how can we not occasionally utter a few groans ourselves?

"PRAY FOR MY ENEMIES? SURELY YOU'RE JOKING!"

ॐ

Praying for one's enemies is no joke—it's exactly what Jesus instructed His disciples to do and what He said applies to us today. "You have heard that it was said, 'Love your neighbor and hate your enemy.' But I tell you: Love your enemies and pray for those who persecute you, that you may be sons of your Father in heaven. He causes his sun to rise on the evil and the good, and sends rain on the righteous and the unrighteous." (Matt. 5:43–45). In another passage, Luke recorded four specific responsibilities: "Love your enemies, do good to those who hate you, bless those who curse you, pray for those who mistreat you" (Luke 6:27–28). That's quite an agenda!

Christians shouldn't deliberately *make* enemies, but if we follow Jesus Christ, we will certainly *have* enemies, and often they will be professed "religious people," the kind of people who crucified Jesus. Some people will hate us, others will hate us and curse us, and a few will hate us, curse us, *and* deliberately mistreat us. That's the way the world ("society apart from God") treated Jesus, and that's the way we should be expected to be treated the more we become like Him. If you want to be comfortable in this world, then you can't be conformable to Jesus Christ (see Rom. 12:1–2).

In spite of occasional bland tributes to "Jesus the teacher" or "Jesus the lowly carpenter," the world hates Jesus Christ and the people who try to live like Him (see John 16:18–25). You can talk about "God" in a generic way in a public civic ceremony, but you don't dare mention the name of Jesus in a manner that suggests that He is Lord—unless you want to be attacked by the politically correct. "They will treat you this way because of my name," Jesus said (John 15:21), but this kind of treatment can be a pathway to blessing. "Blessed are you when people insult you, persecute you and falsely say all kinds of evil against you because of me. Rejoice and be glad, because great is your reward in heaven" (Matt. 5:11–12). It all depends on our faith and love.

If we covet a win/lose solution to a problem—we win, they lose—then matters will only grow worse, and God's reputation and our testimony may suffer. But if by faith we seek a win/win solution, so that we grow spiritually and that we grow spiritually and that

TO "LOVE" THESE PEOPLE SIMPLY MEANS TO TREAT THEM THE WAY THE LORD TREATS US.

our enemies get closer to repentance, then God is glorified. But even if our enemies resist our love and oppose our Lord,

we have a guaranteed reward in heaven that will honor Jesus Christ.
After all, a hundred years from now, it will make little difference what people think or say about us, but what God does
with us will make a great deal of difference.

So, when we pray for our enemies, what should we ask
God to do? Should we read their names into David's
imprecatory psalms and beg God to destroy them? How do
we love our enemies, do good to them, and honestly pray
for them?

For Christian believers, to "love" these people simply
means to treat them the way the Lord treats us. God listens
to us, so we listen to them. God is kind to us, so we are kind
to them. God doesn't give us what we deserve (that's mercy),
but He does give us what we don't deserve (that's grace), and
we should follow His example. God forgives us for Jesus'
sake, and we should forgive others for Jesus' sake. God wills
His very best for us, and we should pray for His very best for
those who treat us the worst.

But this is something we can't do in our own natural
strength. This kind of Christian living demands a great deal of
faith and love, and only the Holy Spirit can provide what we
need to have that kind of love (see Rom. 5:5).

It's likely that Stephen's example and prayer at his martyrdom was a turning point in the life of Saul of Tarsus (see
Acts 7:54–8:1; 22:10), and this is an encouragement to us
whenever people start throwing verbal stones at us—or even
real stones. With our eyes on that heavenly promise, we need
to pray that God will bless our enemies into the place where
the goodness of God will bring them to repentance (see Rom.
2:4). We pray them not into judgment but into obedience.

Not only can the Lord turn water into wine, but He can also turn curses into blessings. The evil prophet Balaam tried to curse Israel, but God turned his curses into blessings (see Num. 22–24; Neh. 13:2; Deut. 23:5). If we have faith and love, we can pray for those who curse us because we know God can turn the curses into blessings, not only in this life but also in the life to come in glory. At least that was Paul's inspired conclusion as he pondered the world situation: "I consider that our present sufferings are not worth comparing with the glory that will be revealed in us" (Rom. 8:18).

The future is your friend when Jesus is your Lord.

"Let's Fold Our Hands, Bow Our Heads, Close Our Eyes, and Pray"

ℰ꙳

If you're teaching little children in a Bible class, or if you're praying for God to bless a meal, this is a safe plan to follow. Children with bowed heads and closed eyes can't see opportunities for mischief, and if their hands are folded, they can't indulge in those opportunities. But as for adults, I don't find any such instructions in the Word of God.

In spite of the beautiful and inspiring "praying hands" paintings, God's people in the Bible didn't fold their hands when they prayed. Quite the contrary, they lifted their *open* hands toward heaven because they expected to receive something from the Lord. "Hear my cry for mercy as I call to you for help, as I lift up my hands toward your Most Holy Place," prayed David in Psalm 28:2, and we find similar expressions in Psalms 63:4, 134:2 and 141:2. That's the way the godly scribe Ezra prayed (see Ezra 9:5; Neh. 8:6), and it's what Paul told believers to do in their local assemblies (see 1 Tim. 2:8). In the Bible, folded hands usually describe lazy people who sit around doing nothing (see Prov. 6:9–11; 24:30–34; Eccl. 4:5).

As for bowed heads, we do find people in Scripture bowing their heads in reverence to the Lord, but the practice isn't always associated with prayer (see Gen. 24:26; Ex. 4:31). God's people usually lifted up their eyes to heaven when they prayed (see Ps. 123:1), a practice that Jesus followed (see Matt. 14:19; John 11:41; 17:1). Furthermore, we're commanded to watch and pray, or to pray with our eyes open. The phrase means "Stay awake—be alert," and probably originated from Nehemiah 4:9: "Nevertheless we made our prayer unto our God, and set a watch" (KJV).

MOST OF OUR PRAYING IS MORE LIKE BEING A SOLDIER AT ATTENTION, AWAITING ORDERS OR OUT ON THE BATTLEFIELD CALLING FOR HELP.

We must be wide awake and alert in our praying because of the pressures and distractions of the world around us (see Mark 13:32–37), the weakness of the flesh (see Matt. 26:41; Mark 14:32–38), and the attacks of the devil (see Eph. 6:18). We must also be alert so we can see opportunities that the Lord opens up for us (see Col. 4:2). While some praying is quiet and restful (like being a child in a parent's arms), most of our praying is more like being a soldier at attention, awaiting orders or out on the battlefield calling for help.

All believers need to cultivate the practice of communing with the Lord while the noisy world goes on around them.

Medieval spiritual directors called this practice "mental prayer." You close your eyes to help block out the distractions, thank God for His mercies, meditate on a biblical truth, and then talk to the Lord silently from your heart. I've done this in hospital waiting rooms, airports, supermarket checkout lines, and a host of other places, and I can testify that it has a marvelous way of calming my spirit and refreshing me for the tasks ahead. I call it "taking a blessing break," and it's been especially helpful when my wife and I have been traveling in ministry. John Bunyan said, "In prayer it is better to have a heart without words, than words without heart," and he was right. "Be still, and know that I am God" (Ps. 46:10).

⅚

This and the previous chapters have mentioned only a few of the prayer practices that can hinder us from experiencing the enrichment and encouragement God gives to those who are serious about meeting Him at the throne of grace.

Now the time has come for us to enroll in the school of prayer.

Semester II

Advancing in the School of Prayer

&

Lord, teach us to pray.

—Luke 11:1

I'd rather teach one man to pray than ten men to
preach.

—John Henry Jowett

"Teach Us to Pray," Entry Level

ॐ

> One day Jesus was praying in a certain place.
> When he finished, one of his disciples said to him,
> "Lord, teach us to pray, just as John taught his disci-
> ples." (Luke 11:1)

If you had the privilege of asking the Lord for one special skill, for what would you ask? Would you ask for skill in making friends, making money, witnessing for Christ, or succeeding greatly in your chosen vocation?

Our answer to this question reveals what is really important in our lives.

One of our Lord's disciples asked Jesus to teach them to pray. They wanted to enroll in the school of prayer, and so should we, *because when you know how to pray, the Lord can help you meet every need.*

No matter what skills we may already possess, we will never rise any higher than our prayer life. The most important part of our lives is the part that only God sees, and the most important words we speak are those that God hears in

> ## WHEN YOU KNOW HOW TO PRAY, THE LORD CAN HELP YOU MEET EVERY NEED.

the place of prayer. "In whatever man does without God," wrote George MacDonald, "he must either fail miserably or succeed more miserably." Failure is better than miserable success, but if we learn and practice the basic lessons in the school of prayer, we don't have to worry about either one.

There are four levels in the school of prayer, and each level has an important lesson for us to learn. We'll discuss these levels in the next few chapters.

GRADE SCHOOL LEVEL: "WE MUST PRAY" (LUKE 11:1)

A satisfying prayer life isn't a luxury enjoyed by the elite; it's a necessity for all who have trusted Jesus Christ. *We must pray.*

John the Baptist was a miracle baby who, like Isaac, was given to a couple who were too old to have a family. He was filled with the Spirit from his mother's womb. He fulfilled Old Testament prophecy, and Jesus called him the greatest of all the prophets. John had the privilege of presenting Jesus to the nation of Israel and preparing the people of Israel to receive Him (see Luke 1:5–25; 7:18–28). What a privileged person John was, and *yet John the Baptist had to pray! And he taught his disciples to pray!*

Our Lord's disciples were privileged to be called by Him, to live with and learn from Him, and even to receive from

Him the power to perform miracles. *Yet they wanted to know how to pray effectively!*

Our Lord Himself was God in sinless human flesh. He could heal the sick and even raise the dead, and He had the Holy Spirit without limit (see John 3:34). There were no situations that He didn't understand and that He couldn't handle, and there were no needs that He couldn't meet, *and yet He had to pray!* The four Gospels make it clear that Jesus not only taught about prayer, but was, Himself, a man of prayer. If the perfect Son of God had to pray as He lived and ministered here on earth, where does that leave us? *We must pray!*

We can't escape the grade-school lesson of prayer: We must pray.

PROMOTED TO PRAYING IN GOD'S WILL

ॐ

HIGH SCHOOL LEVEL: "WE MUST PRAY IN GOD'S WILL" (LUKE 11:2–4)

"When you pray" (Luke 11:2) implies that Jesus expected His disciples to pray; otherwise, He would have said, "If you pray." We may use His sample prayer, commonly called the Lord's Prayer, as a part of our personal or corporate worship—the early church used it in their regular services, and we can also use it as a model for our own prayers, which will help us to pray in God's will.

Most of us are probably more familiar with the version of Jesus' prayer that is given in Matthew 6:9–13:

> Our Father in heaven,
> hallowed be your name,
> your kingdom come,
> your will be done
> on earth as it is in heaven.
> Give us today our daily bread.

> Forgive us our debts,
>
> as we also have forgiven our debtors.
>
> And lead us not into temptation,
>
> but deliver us from the evil one.

Relationships

Jesus' prayer opens with *relationships*—"Our Father" (see 6:9). The word *our* refers to all the people of God, because this is a family prayer for all of God's children to use. You will note that the personal pronouns referring to those praying are all plural: "*Our* Father," "Give *us*," "Forgive *us*," "*We* have forgiven," "Lead *us*," and "Deliver *us*." This fact carries with it some important implications.

The first implication is to remember that whenever we pray, even in solitude, *we are part of a worldwide family that is praying to the Father with us.* The focus of our prayers *must* be global, much wider than ourselves, our needs, and our circle of friends and relatives. The apostle John saw the elders with "the prayers of the saints," not the prayers of *one* saint (Rev. 5:8). We have every right to pray for our needs and the needs of those we love, but our prayers must not stop there.

Furthermore, these plural pronouns remind us that we must not ask the Lord to do anything for us that would hurt or exclude others. I once asked a pastor if he ever prayed publicly for any other church in his city. "No," he replied, and then he added with a smile, "My people think ours is the *only* church in the city." But then he began to pray systematically in the Sunday services for other pastors and churches in the city, as well as for ministries in other countries, and the prayer vision of the church expanded. By including these other ministries in his prayers, his church actually benefited by seeing its members develop an open spirit.

Finally, these plural pronouns remind us that we can't be out of fellowship with our brothers and sisters and expect God to hear and answer our prayers. Jesus made it clear that reconciliation with an offended brother or sister is more important than bringing our offerings to the Lord (see Matt. 5:21–26) and that we can't receive God's forgiveness until we forgive others (see 6:14–15).

The word *Father*, of course, reminds us of the other part of the relationship equation—our relationship to our heavenly Father, who delights in answering our prayers to the glory of His Son. Unless I have put my faith in Jesus Christ and been born into His family, I have no right to call God "Father" and bring my petitions to Him. Effective prayer demands a right relationship with God and a right relationship with others. "If I had not confessed the sin in my heart, my Lord would not have listened" (Ps. 66:18 NLT).

Responsibilities

From relationships, our model moves into *responsibilities* (see Matt. 6:9–10): honoring God's name, promoting God's kingdom, obeying God's will.

Too many of us pray like the Prodigal Son, "Father, give me!" A. W. Tozer wrote, "Prayer among evangelical Christians is always in danger of degenerating into a glorified gold rush" (*The Set of the Sail*, p. 14). God answers prayer so that His name might be glorified, which means that His reputation "looks good" in a world that pays little attention to Him. Before we bring our requests to the Father, we must examine them in the light of our responsibilities to the Father and ask, "If God granted me these requests, would the answers glorify His name, extend His kingdom, and accomplish His will on earth? Or am I just asking selfishly?"

People who live by faith and depend on prayer become a mystery to the unsaved. A few answers to prayer might be called coincidences, but when there is one answer after another, people have to take notice. This is how God is glorified.

When we pray that God's name be glorified, it helps to take the selfishness out of our prayers. When we ask that His kingdom come and His will be done, we become servants ready to do His will and not masters telling the Lord what to do. We're surrendered to Him, we want His will to be done at any cost, and we're praying as Jesus prayed, "Yet not as I will, but as you will" (Matt. 26:39). Nothing can shorten a religious "gimme list" like taking these three responsibilities seriously.

Requests

The three requests found in Jesus' prayer relate to our present needs (see Matt. 6:11), our past failures (see 6:12), and our future decisions (see 6:13). "Daily bread" includes much more than food (although that's a basic need, to be sure); it covers whatever we need to be able to serve God each day. Someone has said that most people are being crucified between two thieves—the regrets of yesterday and the worries about tomorrow—so they're unable to enjoy the blessings of today. For His own children, the Lord forgives past sins, provides present needs (not greeds), and guides us in future decisions and circumstances. So, why worry (see Matt. 6:25–34)?

GRADUATING TO GOD'S MOTIVES

୫୦

COLLEGE LEVEL:
"WE MUST PRAY AS CHILDREN COMING
TO A GENEROUS FATHER"
(LUKE 11:5–12)

Then he said to them, "Suppose one of you has a
friend, and he goes to him at midnight and says,
'Friend, lend me three loaves of bread, because a
friend of mine on a journey has come to me, and I
have nothing to set before him.'

"Then the one inside answers, 'Don't bother me.
The door is already locked, and my children are with
me in bed. I can't get up and give you anything.' I tell
you, though he will not get up and give him the
bread because he is his friend, yet because of the
man's boldness he will get up and give him as much
as he needs.

"So I say to you: Ask and it will be given to you;
seek and you will find; knock and the door will be
opened to you. For everyone who asks receives; he

who seeks finds; and to him who knocks, the door
will be opened. Which of you fathers, if your son asks
for a fish, will give him a snake instead? Or if he asks
for an egg, will give him a scorpion?"

The usual interpretation of this parable is that we must be
persistent in our praying and keep pounding on the door
until God wakes up and decides to give us what we want. But
prayer isn't based on friendship or neighborliness; it's based
on our family relationship as sons and daughters of God. The
parable doesn't *compare* the Father with this surly neighbor; it
contrasts the Father with the neighbor.

Our Lord's argument is, "If a weary neighbor who has
finally quieted his children will ultimately get out of bed and
meet his friend's needs, *how much more will a loving heavenly
Father meet the needs of His own dear children?*"

We find the same approach in the Parable of the Widow
in Luke 18:1–8. If a selfish and crooked judge finally assists a
helpless widow, how much more will our loving Father help
us when we call upon Him? Our heavenly Father never
slumbers or sleeps, and His loving heart is always alert to our
needs and our cries. "Cast all your anxiety on him because he
cares for you" (1 Peter 5:7).

The word *boldness* in Luke 11:8 (some versions read, *per-
sistence*) means "shamelessness" and refers to the neighbor's
desire to keep up his reputation in the community. If he did
not help provide food for a guest in the village, he would vio-
late the basic law of the East, the law of hospitality, and he
would lose face before his friends and relatives.

The New Living Bible reads, "He will get up and give you

> **THE FATHER ALWAYS GIVES HIS BEST TO THOSE WHO LEAVE THE CHOICE WITH HIM.**

what you want so his reputation won't be damaged."

This takes us back to Matthew 6:9, "hallowed be your name." *God answers prayer for the glory of His name.* And He doesn't *lend* us what we need, expecting us to pay Him back. He gives and gives and keeps on giving, just like a loving and generous father. If we pray for something out of God's will, He certainly won't give us what we want, but He will give us what we need, which is far better.

But the parable says something else too: Don't pray only when you have midnight emergencies, but keep asking the Father for your daily needs. In other words, "Give us each day our daily bread" (see Matt. 6:3). The verb tenses in Luke 11:9 (NLT) are important: "Keep on asking, keep on looking, keep on knocking." "Asking" refers to the Father's wealth, "seeking" to the Father's will, and "knocking" to the Father's work. (In Scripture, an open door often refers to opportunity for service. See Acts 14:27; 1 Cor. 16:9; 2 Cor. 2:12; Col. 4:3; and Rev. 3:8.) We have every right to ask for the Father's wealth *if we obey the Father's will and do the Father's work.* The Prodigal Son wanted his father's wealth but not his will or his work (see Luke 15:11–13).

Prayer isn't bothering God, bargaining with God, borrowing from God, or burdening God. True prayer is blessing the Father because we love Him, trust Him, and know that He will meet our needs, so we come and ask. The love in our hearts responds to the love in His heart, and we know that the answers that He will give are exactly what we need. We never have to fear any answer to prayer, for the answer comes from the loving heart of the Father.

If we ask for bread or an egg, He won't give us a snake or a scorpion. The Father always gives His best to those who leave the choice with Him. Our problem is that we're prone to ask for snakes that we think are bread or scorpions that we think are eggs. It's a mark of maturity when you've lived long enough to be thankful for unanswered prayer.

Post-Graduate Work
of the Holy Spirit

ॐ

Graduate School Level:
"We Must Pray for the Good Gifts
of the Holy Spirit"
(Luke 11:13)

If you then, though you are evil, know how to
give good gifts to your children, how much more will
your Father in heaven give the Holy Spirit to those
who ask him!

Matthew's version of this passage reads, "give good gifts"
(7:11), so if we combine the two statements, we have "Give
the good gifts of the Holy Spirit." It's the will of God that we
ask the Father to meet our material and physical needs and
the needs of others, but we must not stop there. When the
Prodigal Son repented of his sins and came home to his
father, he didn't plan to pray, "Father, give me" but "Father,
make me" (see Luke 15:19). He was concerned about character and service, not possessions and enjoyment.

I recommend that you invest some quality time in pondering the prison prayers of the apostle Paul recorded in Ephesians 1:15–23; 3:14–21; Philippians 1:9–11; and Colossians 1:9–12. Notice that the requests he makes for the people in these churches focus on the character gifts of the Holy Spirit. God wants His children to mature in character and become more like Jesus Christ, in other words, to receive the good gifts of the Spirit. Most, if not all, of the problems in families and churches would be solved if Christians were asking God to fulfill these prayers in their own experiences. God's goal for us is that we be "conformed to the likeness of his Son" (Rom. 8:29; see 2 Cor. 3:18), and the requests voiced by Paul lead to that very goal.

THE FATHER LONGS FOR ALL OF HIS CHILDREN TO BECOME LIKE HIS BELOVED SON.

While we're at it, we ought to turn the ninefold "fruit of the Spirit" into prayer requests (Gal. 5:22–23), asking God to produce these wonderful qualities in our own lives by His Holy Spirit. As we read the gospel records of the earthly life and ministry of Jesus Christ, we should be praying that His beautiful character and conduct would be reproduced in us. The purpose of the spiritual life is not for us to become great Christians, whatever that may mean, but to glorify a great Savior by revealing Him in our character and conduct. The Father longs for all of His children to become like His beloved Son. That's why we must matriculate into the graduate level of the school of prayer and ask the Father for the good gifts of the Holy Spirit.

∓

When you review this important passage in Luke 11:13 on prayer, you will discover that Jesus has corrected a number of misconceptions that many people have about prayer.

- Prayer isn't a luxury; it's a necessity. We must pray.
- Prayer isn't bothering a grouchy friend but approaching a loving and patient heavenly Father who never sleeps.
- Prayer isn't borrowing from a neighbor but receiving gifts from our Father. It's all of grace.
- Prayer isn't just for our good. Primarily, it's for God's glory.
- Prayer is not only for the emergencies of life but for the daily experiences of life. "Pray continually" (1 Thess. 5:17). Keep on asking, seeking, and knocking by faith.
- You don't have to be afraid of the answers God sends. He will not give you a snake when you're hungry for bread.
- Prayer means asking for the best blessing of the Spirit, not just for the material needs of life. Both are important.

So, have you enrolled in the school of prayer, and are you making progress?

Semester III

The Internship of Unanswered Prayer

ॐ

Some prayers are followed by silence because they are wrong, others because they are bigger than we understand.

—Oswald Chambers

I sometimes tremble when I hear people quote promises, and say that God is bound to fulfill those promises to them, when all the time there is some sin in their lives they are not willing to give up.

—Dwight L. Moody

Keep praying, but be thankful that God's answers are wiser than your prayers!

—William Culbertson

16

YOUR RELATIONSHIP WITH GOD DEFINES YOUR PRAYERS

సౌ

The longshoreman philosopher Eric Hoffer wrote in his book *Working and Thinking on the Waterfront*, "Early in the morning it somehow occurred to me that never in all my life have I prayed" (p. 118). When I read that statement, I seriously considered writing a book entitled *How to Manage without Prayer*. Then I realized that there was nothing encouraging to say about a prayerless life, so I abandoned the project.

God's people simply can't manage without prayer, and yet many make the attempt. "You do not have, because you do not ask God," warns James 4:2, a text that suggests that prayerless people don't know what they're missing. Prayer is such a costly and irreplaceable privilege that we dare not neglect it or abuse it. As long as we are in this world, nothing can take the place of prayer.

An effective prayer life demands that we have right relationships with God, with other people, and with ourselves. If anything goes wrong in these areas, we can be sure that our prayer life will suffer. We want our prayers to "reach heaven" (see 2 Chron. 30:27) and be accepted by God (see Job 42:9; Ps. 6:9). The last thing we want is what the Jewish remnant experienced after the Lord brought the Babylonians to destroy Jerusalem: "Even when I call out or cry for help, he shuts out my prayer.... You have covered yourself with a cloud so that no prayer can get through" (Lam. 3:8, 44). We want our prayers to get through!

ℴℴ

The Lord not only hears the prayers of the righteous (see Prov. 15:29), but He delights in them and is pleased when His people pray. "The prayer of the upright pleases him" (Prov. 15:8). Every time He hears and answers our prayers, the Lord is sharing His love with us. "Praise be to God, who has not rejected my prayer or withheld his love from me!" (Ps. 66:20). This is one of many ways He has of drawing near to us. "The LORD is near to all who call on him, to all who call on him in truth" (Ps. 145:18). For us, prayer should mean not only delighting in God but bringing delight to God.

A deepening relationship with the Lord involves *faith that leads to confidence* and *love that leads to obedience*. Without faith we cannot please God (see Heb. 11:6), and faith is essential to answered prayer. "If you believe, you will receive whatever you ask for in prayer" (Matt. 21:22). But "faith comes from hearing the message, and the message is heard through the word of Christ" (Rom. 10:17), so we can't ignore God's Word and expect Him to answer our prayers. Jesus said, "If you remain in me and my words remain in you, ask whatever you wish, and it will be given you" (John 15:7).

On the other hand, "If anyone turns a deaf ear to the law, even his prayers are detestable" (Prov. 28:9). The prophet Zechariah further clarified, "They made their hearts as hard as flint and would not listen to the law or to the words that the LORD Almighty had sent by his Spirit through the earlier prophets. So the LORD Almighty was very angry. 'When I called, they did not listen; so when they called, I would not listen,' says the LORD Almighty" (Zech. 7:12–13). Why should the Lord listen to us if we don't listen to Him?

Those who have faith in the Lord have an inner confidence that He hears and answers prayer (see 1 John 5:14–15), and those who love the Lord have a desire to obey Him. Jesus said, "If you love me, you will obey what I command" (John 14:15). They know the joy that obedience brings to their communion with the Lord. They also know that obedience is essential to a right relationship to the Lord, a relationship that leads to answered prayer. The Psalmist confirms, "If I had cherished sin in my heart, the Lord would not have listened; but God has surely listened and heard my voice in prayer" (Ps. 66:18–19). The word translated "cherished" in verse 18 means "to admit that there is sin, to approve of it and do nothing about it."

Disobedience is an insurmountable barrier to effective prayer, especially if that disobedience is masked by religious hypocrisy. In Isaiah's day, the people of Israel crowded into the temple, brought sacrifices to the altar, and lifted their hands in prayer, but the Lord wasn't impressed. He sent this message through His servant Isaiah:

> "The multitude of your sacrifices—
> what are they to me?" says the LORD.

"I have more than enough of burnt offerings,
of rams and the fat of fattened animals;
I have no pleasure in the blood
of bulls and lambs and goats.
When you come to appear before me,
who has asked this of you,
this trampling of my courts?
Stop bringing meaningless offerings!
Your incense is detestable to me.
New Moons, Sabbaths and convocations—
I cannot bear your evil assemblies....
When you spread out your hands in prayer,
I will hide my eyes from you;
even if you offer many prayers,
I will not listen." (Isa. 1:11–13, 15)

Size is the primary measure of success in many churches today, but the Lord didn't rejoice over the temple crowds in Isaiah's day. Dwight L. Moody said that "converts should be weighed as well as counted," and when the Lord weighed the people in the temple congregation, they were found wanting. The hands they piously lifted in prayer were stained with the blood of helpless widows and orphans who had been unjustly treated and robbed of their meager possessions (see Isa. 1:18–23).

Here, then, are four obstacles to answered prayer: unbelief, willful disobedience, neglect of God's Word, and hypocrisy masked by religion.

These obstacles are still very much with us today.

17

Your Relationships with Others Define Your Prayers

രെ

It's impossible to be out of fellowship with other people and at the same time enjoy satisfying fellowship with God. Paul wrote, "If it is possible, as far as it depends on you, live at peace with everyone" (Rom. 12:18).

Surely this begins in the home.

Peter's counsel to husbands and wives in 1 Peter 3:1–7 ends with, "Husbands, in the same way be considerate as you live with your wives, and treat them with respect as the weaker partner and as heirs with you of the gracious gift of life, so that nothing will hinder your prayers" (3:7) Peter assumed that Christian husbands and wives prayed together and wanted God to answer their prayers, so he warned them about marital disagreements.

But it isn't only in the home that we put up obstacles to God's blessing. We can have bad relationships with people in the church as well. "And when you stand praying," said Jesus, "if you hold anything against anyone, forgive him, so that your Father in heaven may forgive you your sins" (Mark

11:25). This admonition ties in with the fifth petition in the Lord's Prayer, "Forgive us our debts, as we also have forgiven our debtors" (Matt. 6:12). Paul wrote, "I want men everywhere to lift up holy hands in prayer, without anger or disputing" (1 Tim. 2:8).

Back in the '60s, I was scheduled to conduct a three-day Bible conference at a church that was about a two-hour drive from the church I was then pastoring. When I arrived on Monday evening for the first service in the series, I was shocked to learn that the pastor had resigned without warning the day before and that leaders in the divided congregation were starting to blame each other. What a great

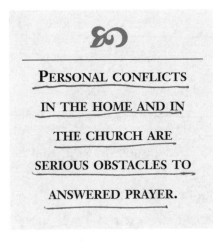

PERSONAL CONFLICTS IN THE HOME AND IN THE CHURCH ARE SERIOUS OBSTACLES TO ANSWERED PRAYER.

way to begin a Bible conference! I'd planned to preach a message on the three "wash" statements in Scripture: "Wash me" (Ps. 51:7), "Wash ... yourselves" (Isa. 1:16), and "Wash one another" (see John 13:14). It appeared that the church needed that very message.

At the close of the sermon, I said, "Perhaps some of us here need God's cleansing and also need to cleanse ourselves. Maybe we need to apologize and wash somebody's feet. If you want to meet me here at the front, then come, and we'll pray together. But maybe you need to walk across this sanctuary and talk to somebody else before you come down here to talk to the Lord." We began to sing a quiet hymn of consecration, and the people began to move. I had never seen anything like it as people hurried to embrace their friends and seek forgiveness for things they had said and done.

We closed with a prayer-and-praise meeting, and the Lord healed wounds and filled hearts with love. *But our praying would have been futile had the confession and cleansing not come first.* Personal conflicts in the home and in the church are serious obstacles to answered prayer, and they must be dealt with. "If anyone says, 'I love God,' yet hates his brother, he is a liar. For anyone who does not love his brother, whom he has seen, cannot love God, whom he has not seen" (1 John 4:20).

RELIGIOUS SCHIZOPHRENIA

ᔕᎷ

P onder this passage from 1 John 1:5–10:

> This is the message we have heard from him and
> declare to you: God is light; in him there is no dark-
> ness at all. If we claim to have fellowship with him
> yet walk in the darkness, we lie and do not live by
> the truth. But if we walk in the light, as he is in the
> light, we have fellowship with one another, and the
> blood of Jesus, his Son, purifies us from all sin.
>
> If we claim to be without sin, we deceive our-
> selves and the truth is not in us. If we confess our
> sins, he is faithful and just and will forgive us our
> sins and purify us from all unrighteousness. If we
> claim we have not sinned, we make him out to be a
> liar and his word has no place in our lives.

The phrase "if we claim" is found three times in this passage, in verses 6, 8, and 10, and it describes the contrast

between what we say we are and what we really are. The claims, of course, are lies, because they don't match up with reality. In verse 6, we lie to *others* about our fellowship with God; in verse 8, we lie to *ourselves* about our sins and try to ease our consciences; but in verse 10, *we lie to God!* To lie to others is hypocrisy, to lie to ourselves is duplicity, but to attempt to lie to God borders on outright apostasy. The longer we lie, the faster our character deteriorates and the more God has to deal with us to bring us back to integrity.

It's the second claim—lying to ourselves—that I want to focus on here. It's a very subtle device of the Devil. He slowly leads us into thinking that our spiritual conditions are healthy when they're really quite sick. We begin by allowing the Devil

> **IF WE'RE LYING TO OURSELVES ABOUT OUR SECRET SINS, WE'RE OUT OF TOUCH WITH BOTH OURSELVES AND THE LORD.**

to deceive us about something in our lives that we consider very minor; then, gradually, we allow Satan to teach us to deceive ourselves about things that are really very important.

We think we're safe because we maintain our religious practices—daily Bible reading and prayer, church attendance, giving, and a measure of Christian respectability—when all the while our thought life is polluted and our secret sins are multiplying. Like the people described in Isaiah 1, we use our religious practices to cover our sins, but the Lord knows the truth.

If we're lying to ourselves about our secret sins, we're out of touch with both ourselves and the Lord, and our prayers are a waste of time because the Lord won't answer them. We've become "religious schizophrenics" of the kind James wrote about: "But when he asks, he must believe and not doubt, because he who doubts is like a wave of the sea, blown and tossed by the wind. That man should not think he will receive anything from the Lord; he is a double-minded man, unstable in all he does" (James 1:6–8).

Revival is simply a return to spiritual reality, which includes being honest with the Lord, other people, and ourselves. It means confessing our sins and stepping out of the darkness into the light.

ॐ

I once gave a series of radio messages based on some of the unanswered prayers in the Bible, and the messages were later published in a book entitled *Famous Unanswered Prayers*. However, neither the broadcasts nor the book proved to be popular, and I wondered why. A friend suggested to me that most people don't want to hear about failures; they want to be encouraged by successes. Then I remembered that the noted Methodist preacher Clovis Chappell had published a book called *Familiar Failures* that suffered the same fate as my book, and it was for the same reason: Who wants to read about failures?

But failure is a normal part of life and is usually a stern but honest teacher, and to ignore it may be to invite even greater failure. There's a positive aspect to failure that every scientist, inventor, and entrepreneur can attest to: what Henry Ford called "the opportunity to begin again more intelligently."

Lucy told Charlie Brown, "We learn more from our failures than from our successes," and he replied, "Then that makes me the smartest person in the world!" Perhaps Lucy should have said, "We *can* learn ..." because the opportunity to learn is certainly there, if we want to take it.

As Christians, we must realize that what looks like failure to us may be the Lord's way of opening up a better opportunity for us. I appreciate the observation of Cheryl Forbes, that "[somehow] we never see God in failure, but only in success—a strange attitude for people who have the cross as the center of their faith." If we examine some of the unanswered prayers of the Bible and *seek to see the Lord and His truth*, then our quest won't be in vain.

PERNICIOUS PRESUMPTION

∞

THE CASE OF ISRAEL
(DEUT. 1:26–46; NUM. 13–14)

About two years after the Lord delivered Israel from Egypt, He brought them to Kadesh Barnea, the gateway into the land of Canaan. Instead of obeying the Lord by faith, the people refused to enter the land, so the Lord announced that He would send them on a thirty-eight-year funeral march that would destroy everybody twenty years old and older, except for Joshua and Caleb. Then the nation said, "We have sinned against the Lord." It's doubtful that their repentance was sincere.

Predictably, this was followed by their decision to go into the land on their own, without God's approval or help. Of course, they were miserably defeated. Moses had warned them not to act so foolishly, but they wouldn't listen. It was all just that much more evidence that they were out of touch with the Lord. "You came back and wept before the LORD," said Moses, "but he paid no attention to your weeping and turned a deaf ear to you" (Deut. 1:45). They experienced

what William Culbertson used to call "the tragic consequences of forgiven sin."

Israel went up against the enemy "in their presumption"
(Num. 14:44), and presumptuous sin is a dangerous thing.
First John 5:15–16 calls it "a sin that leads to death," and
Numbers 15:22–31 teaches that God made a distinction
between unintentional sins and deliberately defiant sins. For
the former, there were sacrifices provided that brought forgiveness, but for the "high-handed sinner" no sacrifice was
available. King David, the man after God's own heart, upon
committing adultery and murder, didn't bring any sacrifices
to the Lord. Instead he threw himself on the mercy of God
(see Ps. 51:16–17).

God doesn't answer the prayers of people who presump-
tuously defy Him and do their own thing, and then expect
Him to straighten things out. The first two requirements for
effective prayer are a faith that leads to confidence and a love
that leads to obedience, and Israel lacked both. Except for
Moses, Caleb, and Joshua, the people of Israel had a stubborn
will that led to defiance, and because of this, they forfeited
the privilege of claiming their inheritance.

THE CASE OF MOSES AND AARON
(DEUT. 1:37–38; 3:21–28; 4:21–22; NUM. 20:1–13)

What Israel did collectively, Moses did personally, and as a
result, he also was forbidden to enter Canaan. Moses was a
humble man (see Num. 12:3), and like more than one
leader, he failed in his area of strength, not his area of
weakness. He lost his temper, called the people rebels,
exalted himself and Aaron above the Lord, and struck the

rock instead of speaking to it. God graciously met the needs
of the people and gave them water from the rock, but He
informed Moses and Aaron that their arrogance had cost
them the privilege of going into Canaan. Instead, Joshua
would succeed Moses and lead the people into the
Promised Land.

Moses prayed that God would change His mind and allow
him to go into the land, but God would not listen to him. In
fact, He told Moses to stop mentioning it. You get the impression that Moses had often prayed about the matter, but the
Lord finally told him to stop. God did allow Moses to view the
Promised Land from a distance before he died (see Deut.
34:1–4), and he visited the land briefly on the Mount of
Transfiguration (see Matt. 17:1–3). But the sin of presumption clearly had its pernicious effect even in the life of the
great godly leader Moses.

There are sins of the flesh and sins of the spirit (see 2 Cor.
7:1), and the sin of Moses was a sin of the spirit. He became
angry with the people, lost his temper, and told them that he
and Aaron would provide water from the rock. By robbing
God of glory, Moses and Aaron robbed themselves of the joy
of entering the Promised Land. The refined sins of the spirit
are just as wicked before God as the gross sins of the flesh,
and they can cost us dearly.

THE CASE OF ELIJAH (1 KINGS 19:1–14)

"I have had enough, Lord," Elijah told Jehovah. "Take my
life. I am no better than my ancestors." The prophet Elijah
was engaged in a "pity party" that was inflating his ego but
not solving his problems. It was only making them worse.

But, before we criticize this great prophet too severely, let's be sure we haven't done the same thing ourselves during some low hour in life.

It's obvious that if Elijah had really wanted to die, Jezebel would have accommodated him; but Elijah didn't mean what he was praying. He had just been through a very demanding time of ministry—calling fire from heaven, slaying the idolatrous prophets, and ending a long drought by praying for rain—and he was lonely, weary, and emotionally drained. Whenever you feel like that, don't make any important decisions—they'll undoubtedly be wrong, and you'll regret them.

Elijah made a big mistake when he left the battlefield and headed out alone for Mount Sinai. He had no reason to fear Jezebel's threats, but he did have reason to fear getting out of the will of God. For the person of faith, sin is far worse than martyrdom. Up to this point in his ministry, Elijah had acted only when the Lord had commanded him to. "Then the word of the LORD came to Elijah" was always his signal to move (see 1 Kings 17:1–3, 8–9; 18:1). But now he was walking by sight and not by faith and was out of God's will, and we can hardly expect him to have known what to pray. He was following his feelings, and they were leading him astray.

Elijah and Peter were both courageous men who failed in the area of their greatest strengths. Elijah ran away when Jezebel threatened him, and Peter wilted and lied when a servant girl asked him a question. But pride was also a factor in their tragic failures. "I am no better than my ancestors" indicates that Elijah may have been comparing himself to Moses (who died on a mountain) or Joshua and Gideon (who conquered idolaters) and found himself wanting. The apostle Peter had boasted that he would be faithful to Christ though all the other disciples forsake Him, but he didn't keep his promise.

Suppose God had answered Elijah's prayer and taken his life, leaving his dead body to rot in that cave. Elijah would have left his work incomplete, for he still had to appoint a successor. And he would have missed a glorious chariot ride to heaven! His prayer was selfish, of course— the kind of prayer we often pray when we're alone and nurturing our fears and disappointments. Elijah needed to be with some of those seven thousand Israelites who hadn't bowed their knees to Baal, or perhaps some of the students at the schools of the

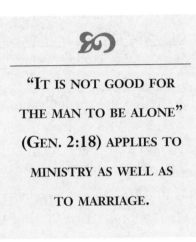

"IT IS NOT GOOD FOR THE MAN TO BE ALONE" (GEN. 2:18) APPLIES TO MINISTRY AS WELL AS TO MARRIAGE.

prophets. They would have encouraged him. Even our Lord didn't face Gethsemane alone but asked three of His disciples to accompany Him (see Mark 14:32–42). "It is not good for the man to be alone" (Gen. 2:18) applies to ministry as well as to marriage. Jesus sent out His disciples two by two so they could encourage and help each other (see Mark 6:7), and Solomon wrote, "Two are better than one." (see Eccl. 4:9–12).

When James wanted to encourage his readers to pray and trust God no matter how they felt, he advised them to consider Elijah. "The prayer of a righteous man is powerful and effective. Elijah was a man just like us" (James 5:16–17).

What an encouragement, especially in those dark hours of life when we tell the Lord, "I've had enough." That's when the Lord draws near to us and carries us through, "for he knows how we are formed, he remembers that we are dust" (Ps. 103:14).

Both Moses and Elijah experienced the pain of disappointment and the rebuke of unanswered prayer. But both of them also shared the glory of Jesus on the Mount of Transfiguration (see Matt. 17:1–3). Let's remember Elijah on the mountain of glory and not in the cave of gloom. Where sin abounds, God's grace is superabundant.

SALOME, JAMES, AND JOHN (MATT. 20:17–28)

Salome was one of the women who accompanied Jesus in His ministry and "cared for his needs," and most Bible scholars believe she was the wife of Zebedee and the mother of James and John (see Matt. 27:56; Mark 15:40–41; 16:1). One thing is certain: She had high ambitions for her two sons. However, Jesus did not answer her prayer.

> Then the mother of Zebedee's sons came to Jesus with her sons and, kneeling down, asked a favor of him.
>
> "What is it you want?" he asked.
>
> She said, "Grant that one of these two sons of mine may sit at your right and the other at your left in your kingdom."
>
> "You don't know what you are asking," Jesus said to them. "Can you drink the cup I am going to drink?"
>
> "We can," they answered.

Jesus said to them, "You will indeed drink from
my cup, but to sit at my right or left is not for me to
grant. These places belong to those for whom they
have been prepared by my Father."

When the ten heard about this, they were indignant with the two brothers. Jesus called them together
and said, "You know that the rulers of the Gentiles
lord it over them, and their high officials exercise
authority over them. Not so with you. Instead, whoever wants to become great among you must be your
servant, and whoever wants to be first must be your
slave—just as the Son of Man did not come to be
served, but to serve, and to give his life as a ransom
for many." (Matt. 20:20–28)

James and John had a praying mother who obeyed the
basic rules for getting answers to prayer. First, she had the right
attitude as she humbly came to Jesus, knelt at His feet, and
stated her request simply and specifically. In his excellent section on prayer in *The Institutes of Christian Religion*, John Calvin
lists *reverence* as the first rule of prayer, and this rule Salome had
obeyed. Second, she claimed a promise, for prayer involves
claiming God's promises, and Jesus had said that the apostles
would sit with Him on thrones (see Matt. 19:28). Third, she
exhibited great faith, because Jesus had just announced that He
would be condemned to death on the cross (see Matt.
20:17–19). Why ask for thrones when He had a cross in His
future? Finally, she and her two sons had agreed on this
request, and Jesus had promised to answer that kind of prayer
(see Matt. 18:19).

Society today is obsessed with "how-to" books with their "seven steps to success," and the malady has unfortunately infected the church. Why seven steps and not ten? What biblical texts gave these authors the basis for using these numbers? One evangelical publisher I know changed a perfectly good title into one with a number in it because, according to the marketing people, "numbers are a big thing these days because people like things they can measure." What ever happened to "the whole measure of the fullness of Christ" (Eph. 4:13)?

Salome followed the accepted rules for successful prayer, but the Lord still didn't give her what she asked for. Why? Because she forgot to balance these rules with what Jesus taught in the Lord's Prayer, starting with relationships. She ignored the fact that she and her sons belonged to the family of faith and that they were asking only for themselves and forgetting everybody else. No wonder the other apostles were indignant, for selfish praying divides the family of God.

James 4 is the "war chapter" of the Bible, explaining why some Christians can't get along with other believers, and one of the basic causes is given in verse 3: "When you ask, you do not receive, because you ask with wrong motives, that you may spend what you get on your pleasures." Salome was sure her sons deserved those thrones, which means she didn't have much regard for the other apostles, some of whom may have deserved the thrones even more.

The concept of motivation in prayer moves us from relationships to the responsibilities stated in the Lord's Prayer. Did Salome's request glorify God's name? Probably not. Did her prayer help to hasten the coming of Christ's kingdom? No. Did it help accomplish God's will on earth? Not according to Jesus. Had Salome and her sons run their request through the grid of the Lord's Prayer, they would never have brought it to the Master in the first place. Prayer means much more than following rules; it also means respecting relationships and accepting responsibilities.

Prayer involves *giving* and not just *getting*. Cheap answers to prayer are really not worth receiving. For Jesus to sit on His throne, He had to suffer and die, but James and John wanted to get their thrones without paying a price. "You don't know what you are asking," the Lord said to them. "Can you drink the cup I drink or be baptized with the baptism I am baptized with?" Their answer has always startled me: "We can" (Mark 10:38–39). They not only didn't know what they were asking, but they didn't know their own hearts. They really thought they could follow Jesus in His suffering, but when the crisis came, they forsook Him and fled just like the other disciples.

Prayer is a gracious privilege, and the answers God sends are gifts, *but there is still a price to pay*. I'll have more to say about this when we consider Paul's prayer recorded in Ephesians 3:14–21, but for now, I want to emphasize this: We must be prepared not only to pray but also to receive the answer God sends and use it to glorify Him. James and John didn't receive assurance that they would be enthroned in places of honor, but they did have the assurance that they would drink the cup and experience the baptism. James was the first of the apostles to be martyred (see Acts 12:1–2). John was the last to die, but before he died, he suffered persecution and exile for the name of Christ.

Is it necessary for us to ask God for a throne when we

are already seated with Christ in the heavenlies (see Eph. 2:6)? Furthermore, *prayer is our throne in this world, a "throne of grace"* (see Heb. 4:14–16). God's grace is reigning because Christ is reigning, and we have the privilege of "reign[ing] in life" through Him (Rom. 5:17). James and John wanted to sit in places of honor in the future kingdom, but we have a greater honor because we are *today* seated with Christ, privileged to come to the throne of grace, and therefore reigning in life as overcomers in the name of Jesus.

Finally, it's a dangerous thing to tell Jesus that we deserve a throne and are prepared to pay the price. James did drink the cup. John outlived all the apostles, and when he was an old man, he was exiled on the island of Patmos (see Rev. 1:9), he experienced the baptism. Even for Jesus Christ there first had to be the cross and then the crown, first the suffering and then the glory, and who are we to reverse God's order? When it comes to prayer, we ask what we wish from God, but we must be prepared to pay for it. I'll have more to say about this in the next section.

There are so many wonderful answers to prayer recorded in Scripture that the few unanswered prayers need not discourage us. If anything, they encourage us to examine our hearts and our prayers to be sure we're asking in the will of God. That is our task in the next section.

EXAMINATION TIME

Search me, O God, and know my heart; test me and know my anxious thoughts. See if there is any offensive way in me, and lead me in the way everlasting.

—PSALM 139:23–24

Examine yourselves to see whether you are in the faith; test yourselves.

—2 CORINTHIANS 13:5

An unexamined Christian stands like an unattended garden. Let your garden go unattended for a few months, and you will not have roses and tomatoes but weeds.... It takes examination, teaching, instruction, discipline, caring, tending, weeding and cultivating to keep the life right.

—A. W. TOZER, *RUT, ROT OR REVIVAL* (P. 43)

If I pray that someone else may be, or do something which I am not, and don't intend to do, my praying is paralyzed.

—OSWALD CHAMBERS, *DISCIPLES INDEED* (P. 41)

Taking Inventory of Your Prayer Life

ɛɔ

D escribing the final hours of Socrates, Plato in his *Apology* tells us that the great philosopher said, "The unexamined life is not worth living." Socrates was right. While too much introspection can lead to despair, and shallow examination can result in false confidence, honest evaluation can make us better people, if we act upon what we learn.

To submit to the Spirit's scrutiny as we look into the mirror of God's Word is to grow in the knowledge of God and of ourselves and to develop humility, honesty, and integrity. To live in a fictional dream world is to court disaster. That's why David prayed, "Search me, O God" (Psalm 139:23). God's approach is tender and His diagnosis is accurate, so we don't have to be afraid. His examination is an X-ray, not an autopsy.

If the unexamined life is not worth living, the unexamined prayer life is not worth continuing. It's very easy to follow a "daily devotional routine" but not really pray. We read our assigned Bible verses and follow our prayer calendars, but day after day, we unconsciously push a mental "replay" button and pray the way we always pray. When we're finished, we congratulate ourselves that we've been faithful in our daily "prayer time," but very little of lasting spiritual good has been accomplished.

I find it helpful to test my own praying by meditating on the prayers recorded in Scripture, especially the prison prayers of Paul (see Eph. 1:15–23; 3:14–21; Phil. 1:9–11; Col. 1:9–12). Paul's second prayer in Ephesians 3:14–21 encourages us to ask ourselves some personal questions about our prayer life:

> For this reason I kneel before the Father, from whom his whole family in heaven and on earth derives its name. I pray that out of his glorious riches he may strengthen you with power through his Spirit in your inner being, so that Christ may dwell in your hearts through faith. And I pray that you, being rooted and established in love, may have power, together with all the saints, to grasp how wide and long and high and deep is the love of Christ, and to know this love that surpasses knowledge—that you may be filled to the measure of all the fullness of God.
>
> Now to him who is able to do immeasurably more than all we ask or imagine, according to his power that is at work within us, to him be glory in the church and in Christ Jesus throughout all generations, for ever and ever! Amen.

Am I Praying?

Paul was a man of prayer. As an unconverted Pharisee, he certainly offered the traditional prayers of Judaism, and his Christian life began with three days of fasting and prayer (see Acts 9:9, 11). He wasn't embarrassed to ask his friends to pray for him (see Rom. 15:30; Eph. 6:19; Col. 4:3; 1 Thess. 5:25; 2 Thess. 3:1), and he was faithful to pray for them (see Rom. 1:8–10; Eph. 1:15–23; 3:14–21; Phil. 1:4, 9–11; Col. 1:3, 9–12; 1 Thess. 1:3; 2 Thess. 1:11; 2 Tim. 1:3). To Paul, prayer wasn't just important; it was essential.

Paul knew that prayer is not a luxury but a necessity, that the Christian who doesn't pray will gradually lose power and spiritual perception and eventually faint and fail. Jesus told his disciples that "they should always pray and not give up" (Luke 18:1). The word translated "give up" means "to become weary, to give in to evil, to turn coward." Prayerless Christians not only get tired in the Lord's work but tired *of* the Lord's work and finally quit. They find it easy to yield to temptation and to remain silent when they have opportunities to witness. It's not a very pretty picture.

"But I pray all day long!" some people argue. "I really don't need a time each day just to concentrate on the Word of God and prayer." Such are the deceptive effects of a fast-food society that prides itself in doing everything on the run.

Do you really "pray all day long"? If you do, keep it up; but remember that "pray continually" (1 Thess. 5:17) doesn't eliminate stated times of prayer any more than a quick kiss on a child's cheek at bedtime takes the place of longer quality times spent together. Have you ever prayed all night, or even for an hour? "Could you not keep watch for one hour?"

Jesus asked His disciples. "Watch and pray so that you will not fall into temptation" (Mark 14:37–38). Nehemiah often sent quick prayers up to heaven, but he also knew how to fall on his face and cry out to God for help (see Neh. 1).

If prayer isn't important in your daily life, confess it to the Lord and ask Him to help you set aside time for prayer each day—*and do it!*

WHY AM I PRAYING?

People have different motives for prayer that are good and bad. Some people make long prayers just to be seen and heard by people who will praise them for their piety (see Matt. 6:5; 23:14). Jesus didn't call it piety; He called it hypocrisy. Charles Spurgeon wrote, "Some people *grow* when they pray; others just *swell*." He also told his ministerial students that longer prayers in public usually mean shorter prayers in private. Jesus didn't die on the cross so that we could impress people with our prayers.

There are other people who pray just to get things from God. Their prayer lists are only "want lists," especially when there are emergencies. After a severe storm, a group of neighbors in a Florida town were cleaning up the mess, and one man said, "I'm not ashamed to admit that I really prayed last night." The devout Christian in the group said to his wife, "I'll bet the Lord heard a lot of strange voices last night!" Yes, prayer is God's appointed way for His children to receive what they need, but there's much more to prayer than bringing the Lord a "want list."

Why was Paul praying? The phrase "for this reason" in Ephesians 3:14 takes us back to the first verse of the chapter, which also says, "For this reason" (3:1). The phrase refers to the point he was making at the end of chapter 2: *the building of the church* (see 2:19–21). Let me repeat the wise counsel of Robert Law: The purpose of prayer is not to get man's will done in heaven, but to get God's will done on earth. Jesus said, "I will build my church" (Matt. 16:18), and *one of the reasons for prayer is that God might work in us and through us to help Jesus build His church,*

The Ephesian epistle is certainly saturated with truth about the church of Jesus Christ. Paul pictured the church as a body (see 1:23; 2:16; 3:6; 4:4, 12, 16, 25; 5:23, 30), a building (see 2:21), a bride (see 5:22–33), a family (see 3:15), and an army (see 6:10–18). When I pray, I need to ask myself, "If God grants this request, will it help to build the church in this world? Will it strengthen and increase the body? Will it deepen our love for Christ? Will it make all of us in the family more like Jesus? Will it help equip the army to fight the forces of evil? Do I pray only for my needs and the needs of the fellowship I'm a part of, or do I think of the people of God around the world?" Paul wrote about "the whole building" (2:21), "[the] whole family" (3:15), and "one body" (4:25). Is that what we pray about? If not, why are we praying?

How Am I Praying?

We find four "spiritual postures" in Paul's letter to the Ephesians: *sitting* with Christ in the heavenlies (2:6), *bowing* to the Father in prayer (3:14), *walking* daily in Christ (4:1, 17; 5:2, 8, 15 KJV, NKJV, NASB; the NIV uses "living" instead of "walking"), and *standing* in Christ against the Enemy (see

6:11, 13–14). Realizing and appropriating our position with Christ in heaven determines our practice on earth.

While watching a televised United States Senate hearing, I heard the late Hubert Humphrey say, "Here in Washington, where you sit determines how you stand." Without realizing it, Mr. Humphrey spoke a profound spiritual truth. If we claim by faith our glorious position in Christ, then our walk and our stand will be what they ought to be; *but the link between my position in heaven and my practice on earth is kneeling before the Father in prayer.*

This doesn't mean that kneeling is the only posture for prayer. Abraham stood before the Lord and interceded for Sodom (see Gen. 18:22), and when Solomon dedicated the temple, he began by standing to pray and ended up kneeling (see 1 Kings 8:22, 54). Ezra and Daniel knelt when they prayed (see Ezra 9:5; Dan. 6:10), but David "sat before the LORD" (2 Sam. 7:18). Both Peter and Paul knelt in prayer (see Acts 9:40; 20:36; 21:5). In the garden, Jesus knelt to pray and then fell prostrate on the ground (see Luke 22:41; Matt. 26:39). The important thing is the posture of the heart, for we must be fully yielded to the Lord and submitted to Him.

How did Paul pray? He prayed as a child of God submitted to his Father's will and as a servant of God awaiting his Master's orders. At the time, he was a prisoner of Rome, but he called himself "a prisoner for the Lord" (Eph. 4:1) and yielded himself completely as he prayed. Our Lord is the perfect example, for He prayed, "Take this cup from me. Yet not what I will, but what you will" (Mark 14:36). When we have this attitude of submission, the Lord will meet our needs.

For What Am I Praying?

As Paul prayed for the believers in Ephesus (see Eph. 3), he presented four requests to the Father, and we need to submit these requests for ourselves as we pray for ourselves and for others.

Spiritual Strength (Ephesians 3:16)

The problem here is spiritual weakness. The inner person has spiritual needs that parallel the physical needs of the outer person, and when we pray, the Holy Spirit meets these needs out of the "glorious riches" we have in Christ. The body needs food, and the inner person also needs food, the nourishing Word of God (see Matt. 4:4). Believers need to train themselves in godliness just as athletes train themselves to be skillful in their chosen sports (see 1 Tim. 4:7–8). Without proper food and exercise, no athlete can achieve success in competition.

Jesus warned His disciples, "The spirit indeed is willing, but the flesh is weak" (Matt. 26:41 NKJV). Peter thought he was strong enough to face the Enemy and even boasted that he wouldn't forsake the Lord, but in spite of his good intentions, he failed miserably. So will we if we don't pray for "power to become mighty through the Spirit" (Eph. 3:16, literal translation).

Spiritual Depth (Ephesians 3:17)

Not only do we have a problem with weakness, but we also have a problem with shallowness. *Spiritual depth is one of the great needs of the church today.* Too many lessons and sermons merely skim the surface of the Word because preachers and teachers fail to obey Proverbs 2:1–8 and dig for the hidden treasures. The church at worship too often reminds us of children in a nursery entertaining themselves with infantile actions and endless repetitions. A. W. Tozer said that what people call "the deeper life" seems deep only because the life of the average Christian is so shallow, and he was right (*Keys to the Deeper Life*, p. 32).

I heard Vance Havner say that if a person wanted to have spiritual fellowship with somebody in the average church, he would have to backslide! The church of Jesus Christ should be launching out into the deep (see Luke 5:4) and digging deep (see 6:48). But most people prefer splashing in the wading pool and laying their life foundations on the shifting sand.

In his prayer, Paul used three words that speak of depth: *dwell*, *rooted*, and *established*. The word translated "dwell" means "to settle down and feel at home." Jesus is not a guest in our lives; He's the Master of the house. It's interesting to note in Genesis 18 that when Jesus came to see Abraham, He spent time with him in his home, but He sent the two angels to visit Lot in Sodom. It would seem that Jesus didn't feel "at home" with Lot and his family in Sodom. Does He feel at home in our hearts? Is He able to fulfill in us the promise of John 14:21–24, that He and the Father will come to make their home in us and share their love with us? That's what Jesus means by "a deeper life."

Paul also used the word *rooted*, which speaks of a tree sending its roots deep into the soil, bringing up the nourishment, and standing firm against every storm. "To be firmly rooted" is what the original text says. What Jesus said about people with shallow hearts applies to many professed Christians today: They have no roots (see Mark 4:16–17). Let the sun of tribulation burn down upon these professed believers and they will wither and die, because they have no root system.

Grounded is an architectural word that refers to the laying of the foundation of a building. The foundation is the most important part of the structure because it determines the size, shape, strength, and stability of the building. An architect told me, "If you don't go down deep, you can't go up high." There's a sentence sermon if I ever heard one! It's through disciplined and believing prayer that we receive spiritual strength and depth.

SPIRITUAL PERSPECTIVE (EPHESIANS 3:18–19)

Not only are many sincere believers marked by weakness and shallowness, but they're also afflicted with narrowness. Their perception of God's love just isn't big enough. Most of us have no problem praying for ourselves, our families and friends, and our own churches, but when it comes to grasping the meaning of "all the saints" and the vast dimensions of God's love, we're completely lost. We lack the kind of perspective we need in order to see people the way Jesus saw them—as a great harvest waiting to be reaped or sheep who are harassed and helpless and being led to the slaughter by false shepherds (see Matt. 9:36–38).

But if our spiritual roots are deep in God's love and our foundations rest on that same love, we will have "the power to apprehend—to get our hands on" the vastness of God's love. When that happens, our perspective will enlarge, and we will begin to do all we can to reach a lost generation and to build the church around the world.

SPIRITUAL FULLNESS (EPHESIANS 3:19)

Weakness, shallowness, narrowness, and now *emptiness.* I don't mean empty church buildings, although there are too many of those, but the empty lives of people who profess to know Jesus Christ. In Scripture, "to be filled" means "to be controlled by." To be "filled with the Spirit" (Eph. 5:18) means "to be controlled by the Spirit," and "to be filled to all the measure of the fullness of God" means "to live from the overflow of God's power in our lives." Overflow, not undertow!

Perhaps you know about the man who was commissioned to raise a sunken ship from the bottom of a bay and tow it to shore. The weight of the boat, the pressure of the water, and the suction caused by the ocean floor all combined to make the task a real challenge, but he solved the problem. At low tide, he put chains under and around the vessel and attached them to large barges. Then he waited for the tide to come in. The fullness of the tide lifted the barges, which in turn overcame all the obstacles and lifted the ship from the bottom of the ocean. Once the ship was afloat, it could be towed to shore.

The experience of this remarkable "fullness of God" begins with the fullness of His love. We can never love as much as God loves, but we can be controlled and motivated by that love "because God has poured out his love into our hearts by the Holy Spirit, whom he has given us" (Rom. 5:5). Love is the first of "the fruit of the Spirit," and it is followed by "joy, peace, patience, kindness, goodness, faithfulness, gentleness and self-control" (Gal. 5:22–23), all of which are manifestations of love (see 1 Cor. 13:4–7). Fruit comes from life, and fruit has in it the seeds for more fruit.

Now for the most difficult question in our prayer inventory.

AM I WILLING TO BE A PART OF THE ANSWER?

Paul closed his prayer with a benediction that emphasizes God's power and glory. Our infinite God is able to do far more than we pray about or plan for, because He is glorified by doing the unexpected and the impossible. But at the heart of this benediction is the phrase "according to his power that is at work within us" (Eph. 3:20). God often answers prayer without the assistance of His people, but also, often *He answers prayer by working in and through His people*. When we pray, we must be available to be a part of the answer.

During the forty years that Moses served as a shepherd in Midian, I'm sure he prayed often for the suffering Jewish people back in Egypt. One day the Lord appeared to Moses and called him to go to Egypt and deliver the people (see Ex. 3), and Moses discovered that when you pray, you'd better be available to be part of the answer.

In Nehemiah 1–2, Nehemiah's brother had just returned from a visit to the Holy Land, and Nehemiah asked him how things were in Jerusalem. The report was discouraging and broke Nehemiah's heart, so he began to pray. In response, God called him to go to Jerusalem and rebuild the walls of the city. God often answers prayer "according to the power that is at work within us" (Eph. 3:20).

It's a great blessing to *get* an answer to prayer, but it's an even greater blessing to *be* an answer to prayer. Jesus told His disciples to "ask the Lord of the harvest … to send out workers," and then He sent them out (see Matt. 9:37—10:1)! Real prayer isn't giving orders to the Father; it's telling Him your needs and then *taking orders*.

A Christian family was having its devotional time, a part of which was praying for the pressing needs of a missionary they all knew. When the father had said, "Amen," one of his young sons said, "Daddy, if I had your checkbook, I could answer your prayers." Out of the mouths of babes! The boy wanted to be a part of the answer.

ॐ

This entire prayer examination is designed to move us:

- ॐ from aimlessness to purposefulness—the building of the church;
- ॐ from resisting God's will to submitting;
- ॐ from isolation to partnership with all the saints;
- ॐ from poverty to riches;
- ॐ from weakness to power;
- ॐ from shallowness to depth;
- ॐ from narrowness to the big perspective of God's love;
- ॐ from emptiness to fullness;
- ॐ from being a spectator to being a participant;

and all to the glory of God.

GRADUATING TO THE JOYFUL DISCIPLINE OF PRAYER

Send forth your light and your truth,
let them guide me;
let them bring me to your holy mountain,
to the place where you dwell.
Then I will go to the altar of God,
to God, my joy and my delight.
I will praise you with the harp,
O God, my God.

—Psalm 43:3–4

Bring joy to your servant,
for to you, O Lord,
I lift up my soul.
You are forgiving and good, O Lord,
abounding in love to all who call to you.
Hear my prayer, O LORD;
listen to my cry for mercy.

—Psalm 86:4–6

In all my prayers for all of you, I always pray with joy …

—Philippians 1:4

Until now you have not asked for anything in my name. Ask and you will receive, and your joy will be complete.

—John 16:24

APPROACHING THE THRONE OF GRACE

෨

When we pray, we come to a "throne of grace" (Heb. 4:16), so let's consider the significance of this familiar image.

A throne speaks of authority, and grace speaks of generosity. On the throne is a King before whom we bow, but because He is a gracious King, we can speak freely to Him and reach out our hands of faith to receive His gifts. A throne represents law and truth, and our God knows all about us and could judge us. But grace speaks of God's love, and that love never changes. In His grace, God gives us what we could never deserve, and in His mercy God doesn't give us what we do deserve. What a throne!

Authority and generosity; law and grace; grace and truth; mercy and truth. Is this concept a paradox, an oxymoron, an impossible contradiction?

Yes and no, and because of this seeming contradiction, our coming to the throne of grace is a challenge to our faith and our feelings. When we pray, we must balance in our hearts the awesomeness of God's divine authority and the blessedness of His bountiful grace. "Serve the LORD with fear and rejoice with trembling" (Ps. 2:11). Ponder that.

There are, however, no contradictions at the throne of grace. Why? Because on that throne, grace is reigning through righteousness (see Rom. 5:21). The sacrificial death of Jesus on the cross has satisfied the just demands of God's holy law. Sin and death are still reigning in this world (see Rom. 5:14, 17, 21), but God's grace is also reigning from the throne, and we can "reign in life" through Christ (Rom. 5:17). "For the law was given through Moses; grace and truth came through Jesus Christ" (John 1:17).

When we pray in the Spirit, we are actively sharing "the throne rights" of the Savior. We come in His name, which means with His authority, asking what He would ask. Because of this privilege, we can come with boldness and freedom of speech, speaking to the Father just as Jesus spoke to Him when He was ministering on earth.

That is why the apparent paradox works. We "rejoice with trembling" because we tremble before the throne and yet rejoice at God's grace.

"REJOICE IN THE LORD"

Let's consider first what it means to rejoice in the Lord and revel in who He is and what He says and does.

When we pray, our fellowship with God should be our greatest joy. Our delight should be in the Giver and not in the gifts. When God is our greatest joy, then prayer becomes more of a loving relationship than a commercial transaction. Like the psalmist, we gladly "go to the altar of God," who is our joy and delight (Ps. 43:4).

If God is not the supreme joy of our life, then our praying will become either routine or selfish, and probably both. Our prayers will become routine because they lack heart, and they will lack heart because we have no passionate delight in the Lord as we pray. When praying is only a religious task, it becomes a mere duty we must complete each day so that we can fulfill our vows and quiet our consciences. "When religion loses its sovereign character and becomes mere form," wrote A. W. Tozer, "this spontaneity is lost also, and in its place come precedent, propriety, system—and the file-card mentality" (*Of God and Men*, p. 79).

This is the way religious legalists pray. They focus so much on following their routine and covering all their requests that they forget to worship the Lord and express their love to the Father. Regardless of what burdens we carry or what problems we face, our first priority in prayer is to worship the Lord and rejoice in the privilege of communion with Him. In short, prayer isn't a religious routine of presenting endless requests, as a sort of a verbal prayer wheel. Prayer is primarily a joyful relationship between God's children and their blessed heavenly Father, a relationship that deepens from day to day.

No matter what we pray, it ought to bring joy to our hearts. Prayers of confession bring the joy of forgiveness (see 1 John 1:9; Ps. 32; 51:8), and prayers of adoration and thanksgiving bring the joy of nearness to God (see Ps. 43:4; Hab. 3:18). When in our praying we submit to the Lord to do His will, He sends joy to our hearts (see Luke 1:46–49; 10:21). When we pray about our needs and commit them to the Lord, He sends joy to our hearts and assures us that He cares for us (see Ps. 94:19; 1 Peter 5:7). Meditating on God's truth and discovering precious treasures of truth will cause our hearts to rejoice (see Ps. 19:8; 119:14, 162). Yes, there are tears and burdens as we pray, but Jesus promises that He will transform our tears into joy (see John 16:20–24).

Remember, the main purpose for a time of prayer and meditation each day is to love God and let Him love us *and to accept His will and be happy with it.* The Enemy has a difficult time tempting and overcoming a believer who is truly happy in the will of God.

"Rejoice with Trembling"

God commands us to "rejoice with trembling" (Ps. 2:11). Reverence and respect must balance our rejoicing, and rejoicing must balance our reverence and respect. To be completely awestruck would make us speechless, and there are times when that's a healthy response (see Job 40:1–5; Rom. 3:19); but to be totally overjoyed would probably make fools out of us, and we'd act like groupies begging for autographs from a celebrity. It would be a happy experience to have a personal audience with a head of state, a famous general, or an outstanding scholar, but at the same time we would want to show respect and act like mature people. If I were introduced to Albert Einstein, I wouldn't shake his hand and say, "Great to meet you, Al!"

Scripture warns us not to get too "chummy" with God or to treat Him as though He were one of us: "These things you have done and I kept silent; you thought I was altogether like you. But I will rebuke you and accuse you to your face" (Ps. 50:21). The actress who professed to be a Christian but called the Lord "a living doll" still had a lot to learn, and so do the

people who belittle God by calling Him "the man upstairs."
David has a word about this: "God, who is enthroned forever,
will hear them and afflict them—men who never change
their ways and have no fear of God" (Ps. 55:19).

Perhaps you're thinking to yourself, "But doesn't the Holy
Spirit within us say 'Abba, Father,' which is an expression of
loving intimacy?" According to Romans 8:15 and Galatians
4:6, you're absolutely right. "Abba, Father" is the address
Jesus used when He prayed in the garden (see Mark 14:36).
But the word abba—papa—doesn't imply a contrast between
intimacy and frigidity in prayer but between intimacy and
abject fear, the attitude of a slave or an insecure child (see
Rom. 8:15–16). God wants us to be intimate but not imperti-
nent, especially in our public prayers. "Familiarity there may
be," said Charles Spurgeon, "but holy familiarity; boldness,
but the boldness which springs from grace and is the work of
the Spirit … the boldness of the child who fears because he
loves and, and loves because he fears." At the Last Supper,
the apostle John reclined next to Jesus in an intimate way,
but when John saw Jesus on the Isle of Patmos, he fell at His
feet like a dead man (see Rev. 1:17).

If I were invited to meet a famous person whom I
admired, I would prepare for the meeting and keep the
appointment. So it is with meeting God in prayer. I'm not
referring to the spontaneous prayers that we send to the
throne all day long like e-mail messages. I'm referring to that
longer period of worship and prayer that we set aside each
day, a time that is set apart just for the Lord. Unless we "take
time to be holy," those e-mail prayers may not reach heaven. Like
the distraught neighbor in the parable (see Luke 11:5–8), we

don't pound on the Lord's door only in emergencies. We spend time with Him day after day, and then when the emergencies arise, we don't panic.

THE DISCIPLINE OF PRAYER

Prayer is a delight, but it is also a discipline. "Devote yourselves to prayer" (Col. 4:2) carries the idea of "persisting in prayer, adhering to it, being addicted to it." The same word is used in Romans 12:12, "Faithful in prayer." This means discipline.

The word *discipline* may disturb anyone who was raised in a legalistic home or who attended a school that practiced immediate and strict correction ("discipline") of all disobedient students. Rightfully they equate the Christian life with "freedom," but some can be prone to use 2 Corinthians 3:17 out of its context just to defend what essentially is their own carelessness. Unfortunately, some of us who want to claim freedom in the Spirit also have a difficult time understanding why we should have stated times for prayer and worship and some kind of plan for our personal devotions.

But *discipline* is a perfectly good word and a very acceptable Christian practice. In fact, the English words *discipline* and *disciple* come from the Latin word that means "instruction." The New Testament word *disciple* simply means "a learner." Such training might include punishment, but the emphasis is on instruction, reproof, correction, and reward. Indeed, without discipline, we would learn little, and society would have very few excellent musicians, athletes, artists, writers, scholars, or practitioners of any worthy skill from architecture to zoology.

Discipline doesn't destroy freedom; if anything, discipline

releases and enhances freedom. "I will walk about in freedom," said the psalmist, "for I have sought out your precepts"
(Ps. 119:45). The people who submit to the discipline of
learning and understanding the musical scales will have the
privilege of releasing whatever talent they possess and play-
ing beautiful music. What banks are to a river, discipline is to
talent: It keeps the river from turning into a swamp.

The best way to develop winning athletes is to put them
under the authority of great coaches who will teach them discipline. Once the rules and principles of the sport are worked
into their system, the athletes will do naturally what the rest
of us can do only with difficulty—if we can do it at all! The
Holy Spirit helps us balance discipline and delight, freedom
and order, the planned and the spontaneous, reverence and
rejoicing, and each hour we spend with the Lord will prepare
us to send better "prayer e-mails" during the day.

WHAT DO WE DO AND WHY DO WE DO IT?

Here are the basics that you will need for your daily meeting
with the Lord.

- ✍ A time when you are at your best mentally and physi-
  cally, and a place where you will not be disturbed
- ✍ Your Bible
- ✍ A notebook for recording prayer requests, answers to
  prayer, and truths the Lord gives you from the Word
  day by day
- ✍ Whatever prayer calendars you use for the ministries
  God has burdened you to support in prayer (and perhaps financially)

✓ ❧ A heart prepared to worship the Lord, to hear Him
     speak from the Word, to pray, and to wait before Him
     in silence

Your daily meeting with the Lord is both the thermostat
and the thermometer of your spiritual life. If you find yourself wanting to postpone it, rush through it, or (God forbid!)
cancel it, then you know you're moving into serious trouble
spiritually. Satan will use many subtle devices in his attempt
to make you minimize this appointment, and you will have
to turn to the Lord for help and determine to protect your
special time with the Lord.

The Enemy's main tactic is to get us so busy that the time
gets away from us and we have no time to pray. As busy as
he was, Jesus arose early in the morning to pray (see Mark
1:35), and no matter how large the crowds of people seeking
His help, He went off alone to pray (see Matt. 14:22–23). If
we are too busy to pray, we are too busy, and we must learn
to say no to the many lesser demands of life.

Begin your time with the Lord by quietly reflecting on His
mercies and thanking Him for all that He is and does and
gives. You may want to reflect on a Bible truth or on the
words of a hymn. You may even want to sing to Him! Each
of us must discover what our best approach is to this special
time, but always ... ALWAYS ... focus on Jesus Christ and
magnify Him.

> The LORD your God is with you,
>
> he is mighty to save.
>
> He will take great delight in you,

he will quiet you with his love,
he will rejoice over you with singing."
(Zeph. 3:17)

Once your heart has been quieted before the Lord and your focus is on Him, you may open the Word and read His message to you for that day. I've found it best to follow a Bible reading schedule and to read from both the Old and New Testaments. Many believers have found that starting in Genesis 1, Psalm 1, and Matthew 1 and reading through the Bible at their own pace is a good plan to follow. You need not read an entire chapter each day. In fact, you may find yourself challenged by one verse or paragraph, but you will be reading systematically at a pace that best suits you. Follow the cross-references and you may discover some of the "byways of blessing" that crisscross throughout the Scriptures.

You aren't engaged in a marathon; you're simply listening to the Lord, so don't think you must read a certain number of verses. Each day is new, each day is different, and each day the Spirit directs us to the verses that we need. The Spirit may also lead you to stop reading and meditating and start praying about something that the Word brought to your attention. Be obedient. When the Lord gives you a spiritual gem, write it in your notebook. You will use it someday in your personal ministry to others.

Prayer Lists

Some of us like to use prayer lists, but we must take care that our praying doesn't become the mere routine mentioning of people and requests. Again, you must let the Lord direct you, but do try to be orderly in your praying. I have a list of requests that I follow every day as well as shorter lists for each day of the week. When I pray, sometimes I follow Paul and "make mention" of people in my prayers, and other times I spend more time praying for certain people and their needs. I usually sandwich the praying between the times I read and meditate on the Word, but our praying must not be limited to what's written on our lists. We must allow the Spirit to remind us of needs, and we must obey when He speaks. Remember, prayer is not a routine of requests, it's a loving relationship between you and the Lord, and while we do well to give order to our conversations, there must also be room for the spontaneous and the unexpected.

It's impossible to pray for every person in every ministry, so we must allow the Lord to give us the burden to pray as He desires. Two or three times a year, we need to examine our prayer lists and pray about our praying. If the lists have grown longer than the time we can sincerely devote to them, then our praying may become only the mentioning of names rather than Spirit-led intercession. I've had the experience of praying faithfully about a matter and one day sensing the Lord "weaning" my heart away from it, so I've turned it over to Him and moved on. Don't feel guilty if you drop an item from your prayer list. Just be sure that your motive is right and that the Lord is directing you.

Prayer Calendars

Over the years, the Lord has burdened me and my wife for certain ministries that we support financially and with our prayers, and I like to use their prayer calendars. Some of these calendars are excellent. They list the names of people (where it's safe to do so) and tell me where they are, what their ministry is, and what they need. I like specific prayer requests. I'm not sure I know how to pray for nebulous requests, like "the girl's basketball team" or "May our hearts be found in the nursery of God," and I'm especially baffled by purple prose "devotional thoughts" for the day instead of a specific request.

Having been associated with a number of international ministries, I know the problems involved in producing and distributing prayer calendars month after month, but that shouldn't hinder the writers from naming specific needs for each day. "The annual Spain field conference is scheduled for May 10–15" tells me where, when, and what, and I know enough about field conferences to pray intelligently during that week. If a meeting is canceled too late for the editor to change the calendar, the Spirit of God knows all about it and will direct our prayers (see Rom. 8:26–27). Prayer calendars should give us cries for help from the trenches, not clever devotional thoughts or *belles lettres* (definition: "elegant and polished literature that is inconsequential in subject or scope").

Devotional Books

If you want to use a devotional book, or any Christian book that nourishes the spiritual life, plan to read it *after* you've finished meditating on the Scriptures and praying. You don't want even an excellent book to take the place of your Bible, and the nuggets of truth God gives you personally are always going to be more meaningful to you than what you find in a book.

I'm always quick to recommend the books that have been around for a few years—or a few centuries! God guides us "in paths of righteousness" (Ps. 23:3), and the word translated "paths" means "well-worn ruts." Beware of authors who claim they've found new truths that nobody has ever seen before. They probably haven't gone back far enough in their own reading. The "well-worn ruts" that can lead you and me to a holy life are the same paths that were trodden by the patriarchs, the prophets, the apostles, the martyrs, the church fathers, and the godly men and women of all ages.

Classics like *The Imitation of Christ* by Thomas à Kempis, Augustine's *Confessions*, *The Practice of the Presence of God* by Brother Lawrence, John Bunyan's *Pilgrim's Progress*, and William Law's *A Serious Call to a Devout and Holy Life* all help to point the way. There are some "modern classics" that many have found helpful as well, such as J. I. Packer's *Knowing God*, A. W. Tozer's *The Knowledge of the Holy* and *The Pursuit of God*, John Piper's *Desiring God*, and Thomas Kelly's *A Testament of Devotion*.

Of course, all that we read must be tested by the Word of God (see Isa. 8:20), but I find that I can learn from people who differ from me in some matters. In fact, during more than fifty years of ministry, I've discovered that God blesses people I disagree with! "Test everything. Hold on to the good. Avoid every kind of evil" (1 Thess. 5:21–22).

᪥

You must adapt the approach I've suggested so that it fits where you are in your own spiritual journey and meets your personal needs. But please note that this approach won't work if you try to cram it into ten minutes of frantic reading and praying. You must "take time to be holy." If a disciplined devotional life is all new to you, and you want to start with a shorter time and gradually increase it, then begin with ten or fifteen minutes; but be sure you do gradually increase it. As the spiritual appetite matures, we need more time in the Word and prayer, or we won't be satisfied.

ALWAYS IN HOLY DIALOGUE

The Christian life is an adventure, and we need to follow those well-worn ruts of those who went before, but that doesn't mean that our life must be lived in a rut! There are always new truths to learn, new steps of faith to take, new burdens to carry, new battles to fight, and new blessings to share. Paul called it "walking in newness of life" and "newness of spirit" (see Rom. 6:4; 7:6, literal translation).

Grasp that image of walking along the path, with God Himself (His Spirit dwelling within you) walking and conversing with you. If you are in relationship with Him, you have to be conversing with Him along the way. He speaks to you through His Word, and you listen intently. You speak to Him in prayer, and you know He is listening to you. This path of discipline (or discipleship) may be well worn, but the dialogue of His Word and your prayer is very unique and very personal. It is the essence of "newness" of your "life" and "spirit."

So … class is dismissed. Let the learning continue!

Additional material on prayer from Dr. Wiersbe is available for download at http://www.cookministries.com/prayer101

Contents of the downloadable file: